Being Better Co-Parents

Being Better Co-Parents

JESSICA CROWNSHAW

For Imogen

*"We begin to understand that to co-parent is to one day look up and notice that you are on a rollercoaster with another human being. You are in the same car, strapped down side by side and you can never, ever get off. There will never be another moment in your lives when your hearts don't rise and fall together when your stomach doesn't churn in tandem, when you stop seeing huge hills emerge in the distance and simultaneously grab the sides of the car and hold on tight. No one, except for the one strapped down beside you, will ever understand the particular thrills and terrors of your ride." —
Glennon Doyle*

CONTENTS

DISCLAIMER

The information provided in this book is for educational and informational purposes only and is not intended as medical advice. The content is not a substitute for professional medical advice, diagnosis, or treatment. Always seek the advice of your doctor or other qualified health provider with any questions you may have regarding a medical condition. Never disregard professional medical advice or delay in seeking it because of something you have read in this book. The author and publisher are not responsible for any adverse effects or consequences resulting from the use of any suggestions, preparations, or procedures discussed in this book.

WHO AM I?

My name's Jessica, and I'm a co-parent. These are words I never assumed I would say when pledging my undying love to my (now ex-) partner, nor what I dreamed about as a child deep in the notions of romantic love and all I thought it stood for. Yet here I am, deeply entrenched in a co-parenting story that has shaped my very essence. It has forced me to peel back many layers of my particular onion as I delve deeper and deeper into who I am, why I am the way I am, and what I can do about it. And this is not a situation specific to little old me. I am now surrounded by more and more people who have experienced the same situation that I used to be in—feeling angry, isolated, and confused about what happened to the perfect family of our childhood dreams. The latest statistics from the UK Government website estimate that there are 3.8 million children living in separated families as of 2023. This equates to approximately 26% of all children under 18 in the UK today (*GOV.U K*, 2024).

So, what is co-parenting? Co-parenting, or shared parenting, is when two people who have children together break up. They then continue raising their children together even though they are no longer in a relationship.

This is us. We are co-parents, and the experiences I've gone through have emphasised the tremendous significance of getting this situation as close to right as possible—not for our sake, but for the well-being of our children who find themselves stuck in the middle. We can choose to blame everything outside of ourselves, situations, and ex-partners. This list is endless. However, this is about us—you, me, our own deeply rooted beliefs, childhood experiences, wounding and all that other fun stuff that makes up our entire selves. The sometimes-scary parts of ourselves that we occasionally forget to acknowledge as we find ourselves caught up in cycles of anger, resentment, despair, shock, and sadness.

To give a bit of a background, I am a behavioural change specialist and have been for almost 20 years. I've always been intrigued by people—why we react and respond the way we do, how we handle change, and, most importantly, the strategies and practices we can use to grow and become the best versions of ourselves. I love my job, the opportunities for growth and learning I receive and the learnings from the countless clients I have supported through massive transformation and change programs. This career was what I wanted from a little girl—to be an "international businesswoman who helps people." I remember saying this from an early age, resolute that was part of my path. So, when I started in my change management role, I felt elated. I was 23, in love with the man I'd been with since I was 19. The world was my lobster. (I know, I know... it's "oyster"... but I much prefer lobster!)

Following the perfect wedding, and after a couple of years of travelling, being independent and leaning into married life, we decided to have a family. If only it was that easy—a seven-year infertility rollercoaster followed. The trials of IVF, negative pregnancy tests and an ever-increasing chasm between me and my husband, as we both defaulted to unhealthy childhood patterns, was what we got.

At the time, I had no idea what was happening in my subconscious. Now, I understand and accept that these experiences finally tipped me into a disassociated and self-sabotaging version of myself. I can look at these patterns and see why and how they played out the way they did. I was clueless, doing anything to distract myself and not feel the visceral pain inside. I went outside my marriage and met a man who was the polar opposite of my husband. He was open with his emotions, and we shared a powerful connection. I fell deeply in love.

I now understand that my role in our relationship was influenced by my own psychological wounds, which resonated with his. A word of caution here: if you feel an instant, magnetic "love at first sight" spark with someone, it might be a sign that past emotional wounds are influencing the attraction.

Carl Jung and Sigmund Freud, two of the most influential figures in psychology, uncovered something profound about our relationships: the partners we choose often reflect our early experiences with caregivers. Those who nurtured us or let us down shape our understanding of love in powerful ways. As adults, we may be drawn to certain people because we subconsciously want to heal past wounds. The excitement of a new romance can be intoxicating; however, while we consciously seek that thrill, deeper emotional needs from our childhood often influence our partner choice. Subsequently, this can dictate the dynamics within our relationships.

This understanding can be a game-changer. It reminds us of the vital importance of healing our inner struggles to build deeper, healthier connections. Working through past traumas and confronting old wounds can create profound physiological shifts in our emotions and energy. As we grow and strengthen our emotional boundaries and sense of self-worth, this transformation shines through in how we carry ourselves and interact with the world. This can sometimes create tension with those around us – especially with our children's other parent – who may struggle to accept this updated version of us, potentially finding it uncomfortable if they are used to a different dynamic.

I often reflect on the saying, "I wish I knew then what I know now," and it strikes a chord with me. Recognising our journey of healing can turn our past struggles into a source of strength, guiding us towards the loving, fulfilling relationships we truly deserve.

In a karmic twist of fate, after having left our respective partners and starting a relationship, I unexpectedly fell pregnant. Our child was born during a challenging time in mine and my partner's life. As I strived to keep things together for the sake of our baby, I became more traumatised by the day. I was full of toxic positivity, engulfed with self-hatred, guilt, shame, anger, worry, disappointment and disbelief at how I had ended up where I was.

A seismic descent into nervous system dysregulation followed. Becoming a new mother and enduring a difficult birth had also had a profound effect on my sense of self and my vulnerability. My focus was solely on feeling emotionally safe. This came at the detriment of my initial bonding with my newborn as I became obsessed with keeping my relationship together. In doing this, I unknowingly created a playground for my unhealed, anxious attachment style. I was increasingly losing sight of my self-worth, confidence, and personal identity. I hit rock bottom, ending up in the hospital, temporarily paralysed with stress and panic and feeling utterly helpless.

When my daughter was four years old, it was time for me and my partner to call it a day. The romantic relationship had run its course, and the co-parenting rollercoaster began.

I did not adapt well to this new existence. I carried deep heartache at the dissolution of our little family and struggled to accept the reality. I was worried about the emotional stability of my daughter, and as a result, I bargained and begged to get back together with my ex-partner. It was a sad and depressing time, and I forgot all of the skills and knowledge I had gained over the years regarding change, adapting and emotional management.

What followed was an incredibly difficult year or so of conflict interspersed with periods of calm as my ex and I attempted to formulate a co-parenting structure that worked. Differing parenting styles based on our own experiences proved complex to work through and, many times, we would fall out.

My turning point came upon seeing the effect all of this was having on my daughter, and I made a promise to myself to do better. I devoted my time to personal growth, understanding of childhood psychology and most of all, observing and improving the lived experience of my little girl.

I will share more of my story throughout this book.

I now look back on my story and am grateful. The many lonely nights with my young daughter gave me space to read and remember my love of neuroscience and behaviours and I started to use these tools in my personal life. I was motivated by the pure innocence of my beautiful little girl who deserves a childhood with a present and grounded mother, free from the adult complexities of her parents' mistakes.

Her need and dependence on me gave me strength and as the fog started to clear, I began to look at myself more. Why had I responded in the ways I had? Why had I repeatedly stayed in toxic relationships? Why was I so intent on blaming others? My ever-increasing understanding of my own wounding and childhood attachments and traumas helped me to find more self-compassion and self-acceptance for reactions I had had to certain situations. I had my fair share of rage to express and expressed it in sometimes unhealthy ways. That river of rage that can run through us is powerful when it has been suppressed since childhood.

To better co-parent with someone with whom I had experienced such devastating heartbreak, I had to summon the courage to rebuild myself. This was not with the intention of rekindling romance, but with the aim of parenting consciously and lovingly, always prioritising the well-being of our child, with healing and forgiveness as the ultimate goals.

It was down to me. So, I took a deep breath and began my most demanding inward exploration to date.

The culmination of my knowledge and experiences is within this book. This book is for people currently co-parenting, people with children thinking of leaving their relationships, and those with a general interest. In brief, it's for everybody—it's meant as a practical guide, but also a gateway into self-improvement and personal growth. Note that this book does not necessarily apply to extreme cases of co-parenting where there is a requirement for co-parents to be in no contact. However, hopefully, some of the techniques discussed for individual self-improvement will apply.

Finally, I am a British woman based in the UK, so I refer to English law and links. However, the techniques I use have also been used with friends and colleagues all over the world.

How to use this book

I have kept chapters of this book deliberately short. I know firsthand the stresses and chaos of single parenting whether in conflict situations or not. I know sometimes we are too emotionally or physically tired to pick up a book and read it end to end. You can read this book as a whole or choose to read individual chapters. I have also split the book into three parts to ease navigation.

INTRODUCTION

Raising children separately is fraught with challenges, especially when trust is scarce and emotional wounds run deep. Preventing these dynamics from affecting the co-family relationship is nearly impossible without a genuine commitment to self-reflection and understanding. During relationship breakdowns, intense emotions such as rejection, abandonment, sadness, despair, and grief are common. Coupled with diverse parenting styles, the ideal of co-parenting can quickly deteriorate into a tension-filled warzone, with our children suffering the most.

We can find ourselves in impossible situations when attempting to look after the needs of our children, creating discomfort for the other parent. I have personally struggled with this, and others have accused me of narcissism, lacking self-awareness and selfishness, among other things, as I attempt to maintain stability for my daughter.

I want to spend a bit of time here discussing the term "narcissistic co-parent." If we judge by the use of the now popular buzzword, as well as all the social media posts, a significant majority of co-parents are narcissists. While the term "narcissistic co-parent" can sometimes accurately describe a co-parenting dynamic, its overuse can be problematic. A more informed and careful approach to discussing narcissism and co-parenting is needed to support the well-being of children and provide appropriate help to those dealing with these issues.

Gaslighting, bullying, smear campaigning, abuse, the list goes on. Is this helpful for the children involved? Or the people who are genuinely dealing with these behavioural traits? Probably not. A more rounded view of narcissism needs to be made more mainstream. Newsflash here—we are all narcissists. In her *Business Insider* article entitled "I'm a professional of human behavior, and I have some news for you about the 'narcissists' in your life," Melody Wilding, Licensed Clinical Social Worker, shares: "Psychologically speaking, narcissism is a personality trait that every person possesses to some degree. Like any characteristic, it exists on a spectrum. We all fall somewhere along the narcissism continuum."

Robert Greene further supports this idea in his book *The Laws of Human Nature*, where he explains the spectrum: deep narcissists lack a cohesive sense of self, thus relying entirely on others' attention and validation for their self-worth. They take everything personally, demand control and attention in their relationships and are expert manipulators as leaders. They put themselves in the wounded victim role to confuse others and draw sympathy.

Most of us are functional narcissists in the middle of the spectrum. We may slip into moments of self-absorption but have a strong enough sense of self to pull out of it. This creates a sense of inner resiliency. Healthy narcissists have a strong, resilient sense of self. They direct their sensitivity outward—in the form of empathy toward people or focused creativity in their work—instead of inward. Without self-esteem from within, we can fall into patterns of deep narcissism. So, we see that the term narcissism is more complex than we are being led to believe through countless references to those who do not behave in ways that we understand.

Of course, there are those people who genuinely suffer from narcissistic personality disorder (NPD). However, this is estimated to affect 1-6% of the population (*Rest Less*, 2024). Given the subject matter of this book, I think it's important to remind ourselves that, although the exact causes of NPD are unknown, the development of the symptoms can be affected by various factors. Environmental ones, particularly a person's upbringing, can play a significant role in NPD. For example, being excessively praised or overvalued by parents, peers or teachers can lead to the inflated sense of self-importance and arrogance characteristic of the disorder. On the other hand, abuse, neglect and criticism can also contribute to the development of NPD, potentially leading to the attention-seeking behaviours associated with the condition. Behaviours such as manipulation and a lack of empathy for others can be learned from those around them early on in life. Genetics and neurobiology can also be important when it comes to the development of NPD. Some characteristics may be inherited, and changes or differences in brain chemistry can lead to the condition's formation (*Mind Diagnostics*, 2024). Most of these are elements that we can influence as parents, highlighting the importance of co-parenting collaboration and being better for our children. I am observing a troubling trend where children develop an exaggerated sense of self-importance due to becoming the focal point of their parents' disputes. When parents contest court orders or speak ill of each other in front of their children, it unintentionally instils in the children a misguided belief in their own significance.

Back to co-parenting, it's important not to hastily label someone as a "narcissist" just because they exhibit challenging behaviours, as this can escalate conflicts and lead to misunderstandings. I admit I have done this myself and understand the temptation to find fault in others. The truth is that, despite sharing common origins, our brains process situations uniquely. Even with the same upbringing and life experiences as another person, your reactions will differ due to your individuality. It's normal to experience feelings of self-pity, frustration, or impatience when dealing with challenging circumstances or people. Nonetheless, you are not bound to these feelings. Taking a moment to step back and reflect can open your eyes to the possibility of change. The key is to recognise our interconnectedness and acknowledge this in others. Instead of blaming or labelling external factors, you have the power to choose a better path. Misusing the term 'narcissist' not only undermines its clinical significance but also risks diminishing the experiences of those genuinely dealing with individuals who are currently on the extreme end of the narcissism spectrum. When we finally learn that a person's behaviour has more to do with their own internal struggles, we learn grace. By carefully avoiding the use of detrimental labels, co-parents can focus on constructive conflict resolution and understanding each other's perspectives. This can create a healthier environment for everyone involved, especially the children.

Indeed, not everyone encounters issues in their co-parenting journey, and those who navigate it successfully deserve recognition. However, most co-parents face challenges and strains that test even the most resilient. The legal system, rather than fostering parental unity, often exacerbates conflict through ineffective communication methods, increased separation, misuse of legal procedures and rigid, impractical schedules. Adults control the actions and whereabouts of children, sometimes treating them as pawns. It is imperative to shift mindsets toward a more child-centred approach. Our outdated private law system seems designed more to profit from conflict than to promote harmony, keeping legal professionals in business at the expense of parental peace.

I believe it is harmful to hold the belief that young people should not be burdened with making choices. Within reason, children deserve a voice in decisions affecting them. Forcing them to spend time with a parent against their will seems counterintuitive and ethically questionable. The focus should be on the children's needs rather than the parents. Except in more complex cases, such as parental alienation, it is the parents—not the children—who must address and heal from the feelings of fear and rejection that may arise from their children's reluctance to engage. Co-parents should obviously do all they can to encourage a connection with the other parent; however, there is a balance to be maintained. The rigid schedules of the past now seem outdated as we gain a deeper understanding of attachment, childhood trauma, and other essential models for raising a well-balanced child.

In the upcoming portion of this book, we delve into ways to shift difficult dynamics and establish more skilful and conscious co-parenting for increased love, care and understanding. These guidelines have been formulated based on my personal story, research and input from individuals who have firsthand experiences with co-parenting. The primary goal of this book is encouraging coherence and harmony. I have also incorporated my years as a behavioural and change manager insights. This is the guide I wish I had had two years ago when I embarked on my journey. Some of this may apply and resonate with you, and some of it will not. I invite you to take what works and leave what doesn't.

PART I: PIECING THE PUZZLE TOGETHER

The initial section of this book is aimed at uncovering the layers underneath some of our reactions, behaviours and responses in co-parenting decisions and interactions. I will cover the principles of a child-centred approach, as well as explore the reasons our minds and bodies sometimes react the ways they do. Finally, we'll look at some of the interventions that can be put in place to continuously strive to be a better co-parent.

CHAPTER 1: THE CHILD COMES FIRST—THE CHILD-CENTRED APPROACH

When co-parenting, parents can often disagree over what *they* think is the right thing for a child. These disagreements stem from our own experiences, fears, belief systems and biases. How often do we ask the child what they are thinking or feeling, and then react in an appropriate and skilful manner?

The Family Justice Young People's Board (FJYPB) is a group of children and young people with experience in family law proceedings. They put together the below top tips for parents to help them think about matters from their child's perspective:

- Remember I have the right to see both of my parents as long as it is safe for me.
- I can have a relationship with the partner of my other parent without this changing my love for you.
- Try to have good communication with my other parent because it will help me. Speak to them nicely.
- Keep my other parent updated about my needs and what is happening for me. I might need their help too.
- Don't say bad things about my other parent, especially if I can hear. Remember I can often overhear your conversations or

see your social media comments.

- Remember it is OK for me to love and have a relationship with my other parent.
- Don't make me feel guilty about spending time with my other parent.
- Don't make permanent decisions about my life based on how you feel at the moment.
- Think about how I feel now and how I might feel in the future. My wishes might change.
- Be open to change, be flexible and compromise when agreeing arrangements for me.
- It's OK with me if my parents don't do things exactly the same. You are both different and that's all right with me.
- Don't be possessive over me and the things that belong to me. Make it easy for me to take the things I need when I spend time with my other parent, such as schoolwork, PE kits, clothes, books, games, phone, etc.
- Let me choose what I want to take with me.
- Keep me informed about any changes to my arrangements.
- Try not to feel hurt if I choose to spend time with my friends instead of seeing you. I am growing up!
- Remember that important dates (birthdays, celebrations, parents' evening, sports day etc.) are special to you, me, and my other parent. I may want to share my time on those dates with each of you.
- Work out between you and my other parent who is responsible for the extra things I need, such as new school shoes and uniform, school trips, dinner money and the cost of my

hobbies or after-school activities. I don't want to be involved in this.

- Remember that I don't expect you or my other parent to be perfect, so I don't want you to expect my other parent to be perfect either. Accept mistakes and move on.
- Make sure I am not left out of key family events. Please compromise with my other parent so I can join in.
- Please don't stop me from having contact with extended family members who are important to me. Ask me how I feel about them. Don't assume my feelings are the same as yours.
- Don't use me as a messenger between you and my other parent.
- Don't use my relationship with my other parent against me, or them.
- Don't ask me to lie to my other parent or other family members.
- Don't ask me to lie to professionals or say what you want me to say.
- Remember that I might want something different to my brother or sister.
- Don't worry about how others see you or what they think. I am what matters.

Co-parents can find out more about FJYPB at *www.cafcass.gov.uk.*

Love, not force, drives the key principle of the child-centred approach in co-parenting, which ensures that the needs and well-being of the child are taken into account in all decisions and interactions. In this chapter, we will discuss the principles of this approach and explore their effective implementation in co-parenting.

Humans have an inherent drive to control their environments, which helps ease feelings of distress and powerlessness. This fundamental desire for control is a key reason why parents may adopt helicopter parenting—a protective and highly involved style where they hover over their children—despite knowing it may not be entirely effective. The urge to influence and direct outcomes is so strong that people often hold onto the belief in their power to shape events, even when aware that control might be an illusion. This belief in personal influence over events is a core element of human psychology, reflecting a natural need for stability and predictability in a chaotic world. As a result, the quest for control, whether actual or perceived, is a persistent theme in human actions and decisions.

"Why do you always boss me?" is my daughter's current favourite phrase. And she is not alone. Even from infancy, babies resist being controlled and communicate their needs in ways that demand parents respond to their preferences. This desire for autonomy only grows stronger as children get older. As parents, our instinct is to safeguard and lead our children, often based on the belief that we know what's best for them. This is usually valid for babies and infants. However, even newborns demonstrate their individuality in ways that can be both humbling and, at times, quite challenging. For example, consider the infants who stubbornly refuse to sleep or eat. Unknowingly, we find ourselves adapting to our babies' unique personalities and needs. My daughter is very clear about what she wants and what she believes is fair, especially with plans that my co-parent and I have made. As she gets older, I've become more attuned to prioritising her needs over ours as parents and have tried to discuss these openly and constructively with my co-parent. However, my co-parent and I often have differing perspectives, which can sometimes lead to discussions that quickly escalate into conflicts. By including our daughter in conversations about whether she stays an extra night, goes camping or on a long weekend trip, we make sure she has the opportunity to have her voice heard. This approach encourages calmer, child-focused discussions, empowers her to feel more in control, and helps us as parents to remain calm and open. The positive impact of this approach is clear to see in her improved behaviour.

Allowing children to feel in control of their lives is crucial. Feeling in control helps them become focused, goal-oriented, engaged, and optimistic, while also minimising stress. Numerous studies have shown that this sense of autonomy is linked to nearly all positive developmental outcomes, including physical and mental health, self-motivation, educational success, and professional achievement. The reason for this is that children's brains work better when they have a feeling of control. This sense of control can be as simple as asking them if they want to wear the red or green T-shirt, over ordering them to get dressed. Their perception of control activates the prefrontal cortex, the brain's executive centre, which then controls the amygdala, the brain's alarm system. The prefrontal cortex enables logical thinking and broad perspective, allowing children to think rationally and expansively. In contrast, if they perceive coercion or lack of control, the amygdala becomes dominant, suppressing the prefrontal cortex and influencing the rest of the brain. As perceived threats increase, their ability to think clearly decreases.

We can observe the stress response in the tantrums of toddlers or the defiance of teenagers, as it activates the "fight" aspect of the fight-flight-freeze reaction. Or the silence and reluctance to engage as they enter the "flight" state. We will discuss this further in the next chapter.

The child-centred approach in co-parenting emphasises prioritising the child and considering their needs and well-being in all decisions and interactions. We will explore how to effectively implement the principles of this approach in co-parenting to give children more of a sense of control, whether perceived or not.

This approach does not allow the child to call all the shots —it is imperative that we avoid stress, unhappiness and overwhelm in young brains for extended periods. Instead, children should be challenged to develop a high-stress tolerance—or the ability to function effectively in stressful situations. While chronic stress is harmful, research tells us that periodic, tolerable stress—with ample adult support—is actually helpful to the developing brain. When children handle these difficulties successfully, their brains become conditioned to cope, creating the groundwork for resilience. The role of the co-parent is therefore to be more of a consultant than a boss.

William Stixrud, the author of *The Self Driven Child: The Science and Sense of Giving Your Kids More Control Over Their Lives*, surmises that without a healthy sense of control, kids feel powerless and overwhelmed and often become passive or resigned. He goes on to further say that if children "are denied the ability to make meaningful choices, they are at high risk of becoming anxious, struggling to manage anger, becoming self-destructive, or self-medicating."

Accepting that we can't make our children do exactly what we want is liberating. Authoritative parenting, which emphasises support over control, values self-direction and maturity over mere obedience. This approach involves setting limits and reasonable boundaries, all grounded in a shared understanding that we're working as a team with our children, committed to doing everything we can to help them succeed. Children need space to develop their own judgement and sense of responsibility. Even small opportunities for control help them build resilience and improve their ability to manage stress as they grow.

The following principles underpin the child-centred approach:

- Decisions are based on the child's emotional, physical, and psychological needs, with a focus on their overall welfare. Not the parents' own needs and wants.
- We take steps to reduce disruptions in the child's life and maintain a consistent routine.

- Both parents actively encourage and cultivate the child's bond with the other parent, irrespective of their own feelings. This supports in modelling a healthy relationship to the child and will set them up positively in their own views on how to relate.
- Open communication ensures that parents inform children about co-parenting plans and decisions, making them feel heard and valued in a manner suitable for their age.
- Promoting a healthy relationship between the child and both parents that prioritises quality time and speaking positively about each parent in the child's presence is necessary.
- Establishing a united front on parenting decisions and rules helps to create a sense of security and consistency for the child.
- As with most things, there is a balance and implementing a child-centred approach can come with challenges.
- Overcoming personal emotions can be hard, but keeping the child's perspective in mind helps prioritise their needs.

It is important to consistently assess the child's needs with this approach, considering their developmental stage, personality, and any unique considerations. Co-parents should work collaboratively to make decisions that prioritise the child's best interests, even if it means compromising and sometimes having to accept that a child has a preference that can hurt feelings and trigger challenging emotions.

However, co-parents may sometimes find themselves at odds due to conflicting perspectives on the child's well-being and level of autonomy. In such cases, seeking the input of a child psychologist or mediator can be beneficial.

Perspective is the lens through which we view the world, our experiences, and events. It shapes our thoughts, emotions, actions, and behaviours. A useful tool when attempting to see from different perspectives is to reframe and use distinct perspective positions to view an event from different angles.

The perspectives model is a way of understanding and interpreting different points of view in any situation. It involves three key positions: first, second and third.

In the first position, you see the world through your own eyes. You experience everything based on your own thoughts, feelings, and beliefs. It's about how you see and understand the situation from your personal viewpoint. For example, when you're upset or excited, you're in the first position, focusing on your own emotions and needs.

In the second position, you try to see the world through someone else's eyes. You imagine how they feel, think, and perceive the situation. This is about stepping into their shoes to understand their emotions, motivations, and experiences. For instance, when you try to understand why your child or co-parent is upset, you're using the second position to empathise with them.

In the third position, you step back and look at the situation from an outsider's perspective. You view the interaction between you and the other person as if you were a neutral observer. This position helps you to see the bigger picture, without being influenced by personal emotions or biases. It's like watching a scene in a film—you're not directly involved, but you can see how both sides are interacting.

Switching our perspectives from the first position to that of the second or third can offer new ways of looking at certain situations, and as a result, understand why our co-parent is saying or doing something we struggle to understand. It is a powerful tool for empathy and looking at problems with curiosity, rather than defensiveness, and can aid in helping to overcome disparities in co-parenting ideas and styles.

To support this exercise, it's useful to physically move yourself to different positions as you embody each one.

As well as looking at different perspectives from the co-parents' view, using this model for the child can be extremely powerful. I often second position my daughter when talking to my co-parent about potential changes to schedules based on holidays or her behaviours, and I find it extremely helpful. The perspectives model takes us out of ego mode and into a more compassionate space.

As the child matures, their requirements will alter, prompting the need for the co-parenting approach to adapt. Maintaining regular communication, being flexible and using the perspective shift model can help manage these changes.

When applied, the benefits of the child-centred approach are significant for the children. When their needs are prioritised, children are more likely to feel secure and loved, which is crucial for their emotional development. When the focus is on the child's needs, co-parents can collaborate and decrease conflict.

Teaching children with a child-centred approach models empathy, respect and problem-solving that will teach them valuable life lessons.

Perhaps, most importantly, the child feels a sense of control over the situation, and as a result, increased safety, and confidence in what is happening.

The child's well-being is at the forefront of all decisions and actions in the child-centred co-parenting approach. Co-parents can guarantee their child's well-being by embracing this approach, providing love, support, and stability even when parenting from different homes. It's an approach that not only benefits the child but also enhances co-parenting and contributes to a harmonious family dynamic.

CHAPTER 2: THE LABYRINTH OF OUR MINDS IN STRESS

It's all well and good to strive for a child-centred approach; however, things may not be that simple. This chapter will explore the impacts of stress and how it can cloud our judgement when faced with co-parenting interactions. We will also look at the impact of stress on children.

When we are caught up in the aftermath of divorce or separation, intense feelings of anger and resentment can make it difficult for parents to focus on the needs of their children. Parents have a lifelong responsibility and, unless there are exceptional circumstances, they need to develop and maintain an ongoing relationship as co-parents. When we are deep in feelings of intense emotion and stress, however, this can seem like an impossible dream. The human brain plays a pivotal role in the intricate dance of co-parenting, setting the stage for either conflict or harmony. When disagreement arises, our brains engage in complex reactions, defaulting to fight, flight or freeze responses—our primal survival mechanisms. A bit of science here as we look at the workings of our brains—the amygdala, acting as the brain's alarm system, triggers this response, releasing stress hormones like cortisol and adrenaline. While these hormones prepare us for immediate action, they simultaneously impair judgment, narrow focus, and reduce empathy, all critical for effective co-parenting. Unfortunately, significant emotional signals such as frustration or overwhelm are often overlooked and ignored. Even resolved disagreements can leave residual stress, significantly affecting a parent's well-being and continuously activating stress signals. Simply recalling past conflicts can revive associated emotions. Many people mistakenly believe that stress is directly linked to the conflict at play at that moment. In truth, stress is a complex phenomenon that acts as a signal for attention or change.

To explain this further, even when parents resolve co-parenting disagreements, they may still experience lingering stress caused by these disagreements. The impact of this residual stress on a parent's well-being can be significant. Stress is the mind's mechanism for safeguarding oneself from future conflicts. When you find yourself ruminating on past exchanges or overthinking certain conversations, you can have feelings of unexplained stress. When this arises, we should reflect and consider, "What can I change to reduce this feeling?"

Often, this stress points to the need for improved communication, clearer boundaries, or professional intervention. Ignoring or suppressing these signals only provides temporary relief and can lead to missed opportunities for enhancing co-parenting dynamics. I wear a ring that tracks my physiological stress levels, among other things. It allows me to see when my stress is activated—even outside of conflict situations, as I sometimes carry residual stress from previous co-parenting interactions. This has been a powerful reminder to listen to my body's signals and take steps to calm my system as soon as possible.

Effective co-parenting involves recognising and managing emotional and stress signals. This self-regulation helps parents notice cues for a calm discussion or a necessary break for self-care. By reflecting on past stressful interactions, parents can gain insights into how they handled issues— whether they addressed them directly or ignored them in the hope that they would go away. When relating this to a child-centred approach, if a child has a desire to stay with one parent because they are having a fun time and want to stay another night, the stressed co-parent will react differently to the regulated and unstressed one. The stressed parent could be more likely to see through a lens of fear and uncertainty and may override the needs of the child over their own feeling of emotional safety. Having the tools to regulate in the moment or the awareness to step away to reconsider will go a long way in helping these situations play out more effectively.

Here is a list of the symptoms of a stressed nervous system in fight, flight or freeze states to help you identify when and if this is happening. These are physiological changes that occur in the body and mind when we feel under threat:

Medical News Today explains fight or flight as an acute stress response that activates the part of the nervous system that controls rapid, unconscious responses.

- **Rapid breathing and heart rate:** This allows the body to send more oxygenated blood to the muscles and brain in case someone needs to take physical action to escape danger. This also causes an increase in blood pressure.

- **Flushed or pale skin:** As the body redirects blood to key areas, a person may develop a paler face than usual or alternate between pale and flushed.
- **Tense muscles:** As the muscles prepare to move, they can become tense, which may cause shaking or trembling.
- **Dilated pupils:** The pupils dilate to allow more light into the eyes, which allows someone to see better and observe their surroundings.
- **Dry mouth:** Constriction of the blood vessels around the mouth means that the salivary glands temporarily stop producing saliva, causing a dry mouth.

A person in fight or flight may feel extremely alert, agitated, confrontational or like they need to leave a room or location. A severe fight-or-flight response can become a panic attack.

The freeze response involves a different physiological process than fight or flight. Research from the *Harvard Review of Psychiatry* (2015) describes it as "attentive immobility." While the person who is "frozen" is extremely alert, they also cannot move or take action against the danger. Freezing causes:

- physical immobility
- a drop in heart rate, rather than an increase
- muscle tension

People in freeze responses generally attempt to reduce the impact of the perceived threat or hide from it.

Another less commonly discussed response, compared to the more widely recognised "fight, flight, or freeze" responses is the fawn response. Pete Walker, a licensed marriage and family therapist, introduced "fawning" as the fourth "F" in his comprehensive model for understanding how individuals cope with trauma and chronic stress.

Fawning is characterised by a behaviour where individuals try to appease or placate others in order to avoid conflict, criticism, or rejection. This response is often seen in people who have experienced prolonged exposure to abusive or high-stress environments, where they have learned that their safety or acceptance depends on their ability to cater to the needs and desires of those around them. Individuals who exhibit the fawn response may:

- Struggle with setting boundaries and saying no.
- Prioritise others' needs over their own, often to their own detriment.
- Have difficulty identifying their own wants and needs.
- Engage in people-pleasing behaviours.
- Feel a sense of guilt or anxiety when they consider putting their own needs first.

The fawn response can be a survival strategy that develops over time, especially in childhood, as a way to navigate unsafe or unpredictable environments. It is a form of adaptation to circumstances where asserting oneself (fight), escaping (flight) or becoming immobile (freeze) may not be safe or effective options.

The activation of these nervous system responses occurs in times of perceived danger and conflict. Having an awareness of them and understanding our own responses can help in putting in place effective coping strategies, such as removing oneself from the situation or conversation, taking long, deep breaths and moving the body. You can find some other interventions listed at the end of this chapter.

These stress responses apply to all, including children, and so when a child is in a dysregulated nervous system, watching and observing any of these symptoms can help co-parents take action to calm their child's system as a matter of priority. A dysregulated nervous system can be indicated by a screaming and confrontational child or a silent and withdrawn child, rather than just assuming it is attributed to personality.

Children with dysregulated nervous systems may exhibit signs of emotional instability, such as frequent outbursts, anxiety or difficulties with attention and social interactions. These symptoms stem from their nervous system's inability to handle stress appropriately, affecting how they process and respond to their environment. It's crucial for parents and caregivers to understand that these behaviours are not intentional but rather manifestations of underlying challenges. Effective support strategies include creating a calm and structured environment, consistent routines and activities that promote relaxation and emotional regulation. Therapeutic interventions, such as occupational or play therapy or counselling, can also be beneficial in helping children develop the skills necessary to manage their responses more effectively.

I find that my daughter is often in a dysregulated state when dealing with the transition between houses. I always make sure that when she comes back, we put loud music on and dance and jump and sing. We have lots of cuddles, attentive conversation, and quality time together, whether taking her for dinner, watching a film or just playing with her toys. It really helps to fast-track her back to her emotional safety zone. Children who are in the midst of a co-parenting dynamic undoubtedly face challenges when trying to navigate through emotions that they may not be fully equipped to handle. This highlights further the need for co-parents to team together, put aside their differences and help support struggling children as best they can.

For ourselves, we must remember that hyper-attentiveness to stress signals can also be detrimental, leading to excessive stress responses. Learning to recalibrate these responses can significantly reduce stress and improve interactions and overall relationships. Just as people can misuse medication for physical ailments, they can also misapply techniques like mindfulness to co-parenting stress if not used appropriately. The challenge is to find peace in the mind and navigate co-parenting towards a harmonious collaboration. The problem and its solutions are equally intricate and multifaceted.

Techniques such as mindfulness, energy healing and structured communication strategies like active listening and the use of "I" statements can help ground co-parents in the present, fostering thoughtful responses rather than impulsive reactions. These techniques help quiet the amygdala and activate the prefrontal cortex, enhancing empathy and reducing defensiveness. When it comes to difficult interactions, the ability to pause before reacting is extremely valuable. In this space, co-parents can thoughtfully explore their choices and develop alternative strategies for dealing with the complex dynamics involved. Co-parents must develop their instincts to also effectively react in the fast-paced and unpredictable world of parenting.

Implementing structured plans and agreements can further support co-parenting. Revisiting these plans ensures they remain relevant and effective as children grow and their needs develop.

When the path becomes too difficult, professional mediators or therapists can provide essential guidance, addressing underlying concerns and facilitating plans that prioritise the child's best interests.

Co-parenting is ultimately a transformative journey, converting conflict into cooperation and discord into dialogue. It requires an understanding of the workings of our own minds to harness our emotional responses and communicate with intention and compassion.

To aid in managing stress responses, central nervous system regulation exercises can be particularly beneficial for us as co-parents. Techniques like deep breathing, progressive muscle relaxation and mindfulness meditation help calm the body and mind, especially during triggering interactions. Some specific techniques include the following:

- **Deep breathing**: Also known as diaphragmatic breathing, this technique involves taking slow, deep breaths through the nose, allowing the belly to rise, and then exhaling slowly through the mouth. This type of breathing can activate the parasympathetic nervous system, which helps calm the body's stress response.
- **Progressive muscle relaxation:** This involves tensing and then relaxing different muscle groups in the body. Start from the toes and work your way up to the head, holding the tension for a few seconds and then releasing it. This can help reduce physical tension and stress.
- **Mindfulness meditation**: Sit quietly and focus on your breath, a word, or a phrase. When your mind wanders, gently bring your attention back to the focus point. Mindfulness can help you stay present and reduce the impact of stressors.
- **Guided imagery:** Visualise a peaceful scene or experience in your mind. Engage all your senses to make it as vivid as possible. This mental escape can provide a break from stress and promote relaxation.
- **Autogenic training**: Repeat calming phrases to yourself, such as 'My arms are heavy and warm' and visualise the associated feelings. This self-suggestion technique can help induce a state of relaxation.
- **The 5-4-3-2-1 grounding technique:** Identify and focus on five things you can see, four things you can touch, three things you can hear, two things you can smell and one thing you can taste. This can help ground you in the present moment and divert attention away from stressors.

- **Yoga and Tai Chi:** These practices combine physical postures, breathing exercises and meditation to help soothe the nervous system.
- **Bilateral stimulation:** Engage both sides of the body through rhythmic, side-to-side movements, such as walking, tapping feet alternately or gently swaying. This can help process stress and promote emotional balance. For children, crossing arms and tapping the shoulders will create the same effect.
- **Box breathing:** Inhale for a count of four, hold the breath for a count of four, exhale for a count of four, and then hold the breath out for a count of four. This controlled breathing can help regulate the nervous system.
- **Vagus nerve stimulation:** The vagus nerve is a key part of the parasympathetic nervous system. Stimulate it by splashing cold water on your face, gargling with water, singing or humming. These actions can help trigger a relaxation response.

It's important for us to practice these exercises regularly, not just in moments of acute stress, to build resilience and improve our ability to regulate our nervous system responses. By incorporating these techniques into our daily routines, we can better manage stress and approach co-parenting challenges with a greater sense of calm and clarity.

You can also use breathing techniques with children. The breathing we want children to do is deep belly breaths, not shallow chest breaths. When they breathe in, their belly should expand, and when they breathe out, their belly should contract. Some examples of exercises that help children learn deep breathing are:

- breathing in, pretending to smell a flower.
- breathing out, pretending to blow out a candle.
- slowly inflating a balloon.

CHAPTER 3: THE STAGES OF LOSS

During every change management project, we use the Kübler-Ross Change Curve (Fig. 1), also referred to as the five stages of grief and loss. This model helps us understand why different groups of people respond to change in certain ways, allowing us to implement the most relevant interventions to support them. Although I previously associated this cycle with work, when I faced the monumental task of co-parenting amidst heartbreak, it reminded me of the reasons behind my own behaviours and helped me find compassion for myself.

As co-parents, we must navigate not only the coordination of separate lives but also the emotional toll that can debilitate us following a relationship breakdown, complicating both parenting duties and everyday functioning. Understanding the stages of change or loss can provide insight into feelings and subsequent reactions. Note that there are many adaptations of this model:

Shock or denial: The sense that it's not real characterises this initial stage, keeping the truth hidden from family and friends, and refusing to confront the truth.

When a relationship ends, it can leave us in a state of shock, making us feel absent-minded and in disbelief.

The fear of being alone in the future can contribute to denial. Overcoming fears can feel daunting and overwhelming.

We may experience a rollercoaster of emotions and mood shifts, oscillating between numbness and overwhelming emotional outbursts, with the desire to scream and shout. The overall feeling is one of emotional intensity and a disconnection from reality. Panic and anxiety commonly arise as the psyche refuses to accept the changes brought by separation. Often, we dedicate ourselves to work or practical tasks to distract ourselves.

Anger: This stage is often associated with overreacting and acting irrationally. Co-parents may feel helpless and respond with impatience and aggression.

Co-parents may exhibit explosive anger, shifting between hatred and revenge, as well as feelings of sadness and insecurity. The intensity of these emotions can be terrifying.

Expressing anger might be challenging for the co-parent who left the relationship because of the accompanying guilt. For those who are left, anger may be difficult to express for fear of pushing the other person further away.

Anger is often a precursor to the act of letting go. Practical endeavours and mindfulness practices can help redirect anger. It is never healthy to suppress anger or to express it aggressively. Keeping anger inside can lead to feelings of depression and result in chronic illness. Gabor Maté mentions in his book *When the Body Says No: The Cost of Hidden Stress* that "sometimes the biggest impetus to healing can come from jump-starting the immune system with a burst of long-suppressed anger." Keep in mind that anger is often a defence mechanism that hides deeper emotions of hurt, sadness and betrayal.

Bargaining: Thinking that maybe there could be a second chance if the other could change or knew how much the other cared for them.

In this scenario, one co-parent tries to bargain with the other, hoping to restore the previous state or eliminate their pain. It's crucial to recognise that this is not the appropriate emotional state for making deals. Co-parents sometimes make things worse by making unattainable promises.

If you find yourself in this stage, I urge you to ask yourselves the following questions honestly:

- Did you feel valued and prioritised, not perfectly, but consistently?
- Did you feel respected?
- Were your boundaries honoured or dismissed?
- Did the other take accountability when they hurt you unintentionally, or did you get blamed ("You're too sensitive," "I'm never good enough for you," etc)?
- Did your feelings and perspectives matter to them?

When answering these questions, make sure to give yourself time and space to remember, as our realities can be distorted during times of loss or grief. These questions can help you establish if the bargaining you are attempting is valid for long-lasting happiness. I found myself bouncing back into the bargaining stage. Having been in co-dependent relationships since I was 19, I was so afraid of being alone and the impact I imagined it would have on my daughter that I begged my co-parent to reconsider and remain a family. When asking myself these questions, I realised I was not approaching the situation from a healthy sense of self. It took time, though, and a relentless number of rejections before I finally found acceptance. If you find yourself in a similar situation, take the time to reflect on what you are truly seeking. Remember that rejection becomes welcome when we recognise it as a mechanism saving us from a path that isn't meant for us at that time.

Depression: In the depression stage, individuals may experience uncontrollable crying, loss of interest, poor sleep, difficulty thinking, withdrawal and isolation.

It's completely normal to experience feelings of loneliness, sadness, or depression during this tough period. The burden of carrying the emotions of sorrow and loss, along with the significance it holds for co-parenting, can be a heavy one to bear. Co-parents could also face sleep difficulties and emotional exhaustion. The close association between identity and relationships can create a significant challenge for co-parents in perceiving themselves as complete and distinct individuals outside of their previous relationship. Having low self-esteem can make it difficult to perform daily tasks.

Sigmund Freud's description of depression as being "anger turned inward" was helpful to me. If you find yourself full of negative self-talk, self-condemnation, and self-blame, you may well be in the stage of depression. Much of the time, co-parents may have the urge to cry. If feelings of depression persist or intensify, seeking professional help may be advisable.

Acceptance: In the acceptance stage, we reach a point where we can acknowledge both the positive and negative aspects of our relationship. Co-parents may find increased emotional resilience and hopeful aspirations for their respective futures.

This stage has the potential to be a transformative period for some, while for others it may fall short of expectations. Relationships between separated parents can settle down, although, as this book endeavours to highlight, it is also possible that problems with children may arise.

Co-parents might find themselves feeling overwhelmed by their emotions at every stage of the cycle, making them question their sanity. Studies show that accepting and discussing these emotions with close friends and family is important during the painful transition. Although it won't remove the pain entirely, comprehending the stages may assist co-parents in realising their normalcy.

We go through each stage at various times, and it's not a linear process. It serves as a helpful reminder that what you're experiencing is normal and the pain will lessen. Co-parents, especially the one who was left, may find the idea of spending time apart from their children completely counterintuitive. Being separated from a child during unique events like Christmas and birthdays can trigger a range of emotions. You may find yourself back in the cycle as you experience emotions such as anger, resentment, grief, despair, and sadness.

Reflecting on the reasons behind the relationship's breakdown and understanding the subtleties of our reactions can help us align our efforts to be our best selves. This introspection benefits not only us as the parents but also positively affects the children involved.

THE KÜBLER-ROSS CHANGE MODEL

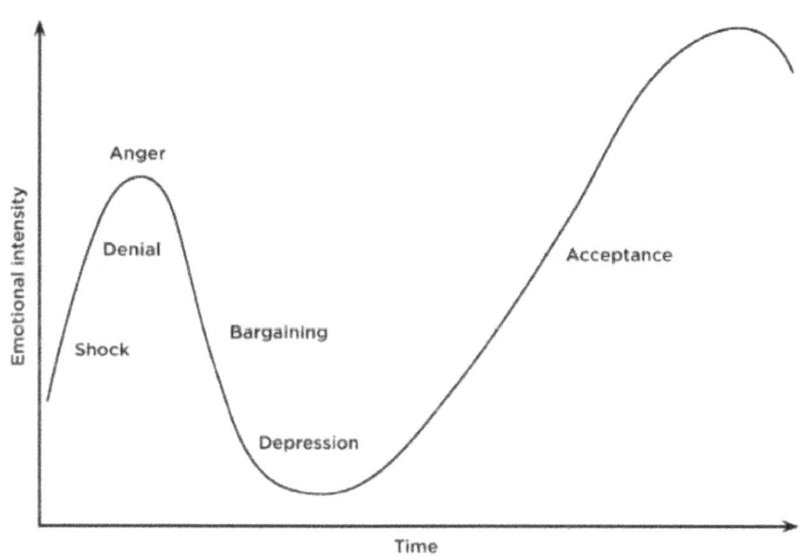

Fig 1: The Kubler-Ross Change Curve (1969)

CHAPTER 4: EMOTIONS IN OUR BODIES

In his book *Healing Back Pain: The Mind-Body Connection*, John E Sarno states, "There's nothing like a little physical pain to keep your mind off your emotional problems." Here, he highlights an interesting aspect of human psychology. He suggests that physical pain can sometimes serve as a distraction from emotional distress.

Our minds and bodies are deeply interconnected. When we experience emotional problems, such as stress, anxiety or sadness, our bodies can react in numerous ways. Sometimes, this emotional turmoil can manifest as physical pain. This condition is called psychosomatic pain. Physical pain can divert our attention from emotional suffering. Focusing on a physical ailment occupies our minds with the immediate, tangible sensation of pain. This can temporarily shift our focus away from more abstract and often overwhelming emotional issues.

Physical pain demands immediate attention. It is a clear signal from our body that something is wrong, and it often requires us to act, whether it's resting, seeking medical help, or simply acknowledging the pain. Emotional problems can be complex and difficult to address. Physical pain, on the other hand, is more straightforward. It is easier to understand and manage, even if it's uncomfortable.

While physical pain might offer a temporary distraction, it's crucial to address emotional problems directly. Ignoring or suppressing emotional issues can lead to more significant problems. Seeking support from friends, family, or professionals, and engaging in healthy coping strategies can help manage and resolve emotional distress.

Some of the most common symptoms of emotional pain manifesting as physical symptoms may include:

- **Backache**: The most generic form of emotional distress is often chronic back pain.
- **Headaches**: Persistent headaches or migraines can be a sign of stress, anxiety, or depression.
- **Muscle pain**: Tension and pain, especially in the neck and shoulders, are often associated with emotional stress.
- **Stomach issues**: Emotional distress can lead to gastrointestinal problems like nausea, diarrhoea, or stomach-aches.
- **Fatigue**: Chronic tiredness or fatigue can be a symptom of depression or anxiety.
- **Chest pain**: A heavy feeling in the chest or chest pain may indicate anxiety or panic attacks.
- **Joint pain**: Depression and stress can cause inflammation, leading to joint pain.
- **Dizziness**: Feeling lightheaded or dizzy can be a physical manifestation of emotional stress.

There are, of course, other symptoms that can cover up and distract from emotional distress. Often, with chronic conditions, there is a more subconscious pattern at play.

Addressing these physical symptoms often requires tackling the underlying emotional issues first.

Seeking support from healers and mental health professionals can be a crucial step in managing both emotional and physical pain.

In traditional Chinese medicine (TCM), practitioners believe that specific organs in the body are intricately linked to emotions. This integrated approach suggests that emotional imbalances can affect physical health and vice versa. Here are the primary associations between emotions and organs in TCM:

- **Anger**: Linked to the liver. Excessive anger can disrupt the liver's function, leading to symptoms like headaches, dizziness, and menstrual pain.
- **Fear**: Associated with the kidneys. Chronic fear can weaken the kidneys, potentially causing issues like lower back pain and urinary problems.
- **Joy**: Connected to the heart. While joy is generally positive, excessive excitement or lack of joy can affect the heart, leading to palpitations or insomnia.
- **Sadness and grief**: Related to the lungs. Prolonged sadness or grief can impair lung function, resulting in symptoms like shortness of breath and fatigue.
- **Worry**: Tied to the spleen. Excessive worry or overthinking can weaken the spleen, causing digestive issues and fatigue.

This approach in TCM emphasises the importance of balancing these emotions to maintain overall health.

In the journey of healing from relationship breakdowns and navigating the complexities of co-parenting conflicts, it is crucial to acknowledge and process your emotions rather than suppress them. Suppressing emotions can lead to significant physical pain and health issues, as the body often manifests unresolved emotional distress through symptoms as outlined above. The key is to express these emotions in a healthy way, and then let them go so they do not fester or build into something more unmanageable.

The way we feel affects how we get on with others, including our children. When we are under stress or feeling unpleasant emotions, we are less likely to be calm and consistent with either our co-parent or our children. When energy levels and concentration are affected, parents may have less to do with their children, supervise them less or be more irritable and impatient. By allowing yourself to feel and express your emotions, you create a pathway for genuine healing and personal growth. This emotional honesty not only helps in alleviating physical symptoms but also fosters healthier relationships with your co-parent and children. Life is filled with frustrations, pain and loss and we cannot control the way that others behave towards us. When we are able to control our reactions and emotions, we enter a powerful state of being that enables us to cope regardless of what is thrown at us.

Beliefs about ourselves are the precursor to thoughts that then determine our emotional states. If we experience negative self-talk where we put ourselves down and criticise ourselves, then this will lead to more unpleasant emotions.

Catching this negative self-talk and turning it into positive takes practice, dedication, and courage. Once you become aware of your own internal narrative, you may be surprised by how often you criticise yourself and put yourself down. This is an easier-said-than-done process as we all have automatic thoughts that just seem to appear in our minds, almost as if they are a reflex; this is our autopilot brain. These thoughts are interpretations of all the experiences and events that have happened to us. We often think of these thoughts as facts or truth, when in reality they are a combination of our beliefs, experiences, and biases we have had since birth. The things we say to ourselves have the power to make us feel calmer or more stressed.

Challenging these automatic thoughts is possible by asking ourselves questions to guide and evaluate them, as well as using techniques for reprogramming our subconscious minds:

- "Is there any evidence for this thought?"
- "What evidence supports this idea?"
- "What evidence is there against this idea?"
- "What is the worst that could happen?"
- "What is the best that could happen?"
- "What happens if I believe this thought?"
- "What might happen if I change my thinking?"
- "What would I say to my friend if they were experiencing this same situation?"

It will take time and effort to reprogramme from automatic negative thoughts to a more positive and helpful mindset.

Targeted affirmations can help greatly in reprogramming our brains to speak more kindly about ourselves, ultimately leading to us feeling more positive about ourselves. Some examples of affirmations could be:

- "I can do this."
- "I've made it through this before."
- "I am calm."
- "I feel relaxed."
- "I am doing the best I can."
- "I love and respect myself."
- "I am always working on myself and my healing."
- "I know I am going to be alright."

Plus, a million others. Choose words that suit your situation and personal style and keep reinforcing your positive self-image. When encountering a tricky situation with your co-parent or child and managing to come through it with a mature and emotionally intelligent response, reinforce your success with yourself, "I did it!"

Remember, addressing emotions head-on and consciously looking at the way you think can lead to a more balanced and fulfilling life, free from the physical burdens that suppressed feelings can impose. Embracing our emotional journey is a powerful step towards healing and building a harmonious co-parenting relationship.

A brief note here on our subconscious minds. Our subconscious has access to limitless information. The quality of information in it relates to how we direct it. Many people unconsciously direct it to produce weak results. For example, you may say, "What if it doesn't work out," and your subconscious will then show you why it will not work. Backing up what you are telling it. This is why it is so important to be aware of how we are influencing our own minds. If we say, "Guide me to the best-case scenario," you may be surprised at the results. Our internal narrative and what we tell ourselves can guide the way we live our lives.

Consider trying the following exercises to support reprogramming your subconscious with more helpful information:

1. As you fall asleep, focus on feeling the emotion of what you want to create in your life. The subconscious mind communicates through feelings, and as you drift into sleep, your brain moves into the theta state—where the subconscious is most receptive.
2. Reinforce your new thought or habit through repetition. Neurons that activate together, wire together. The more consistently you practice a new behaviour, action, or thought, the more it becomes ingrained in your subconscious mind.
3. Do something you have never done before. When you do this, your mind has no choice but to make new connections. In the brain, the unknown is where we can create profound change.

The upcoming chapters of this book will continue to explore the practical and emotional aspects to consider as you begin this potentially challenging journey.

CHAPTER 5: OVERCOMING EMOTIONAL BARRIERS

When a romantic relationship ends, parents may encounter emotional obstacles that hinder successful co-parenting. This chapter aims to encourage a collaborative and supportive co-parenting environment by tackling barriers and presenting strategies to overcome them. Co-parenting can be challenging when the mourning of the family unit's dissolution takes precedence. It is important to stress that it's OK to be sad with the reality and that life has taken this turn. Emotional upset and triggering are inevitable and can be overwhelming.

When there are negative feelings like anger and resentment towards the other parent, it can lead to unproductive interactions and hostility. I myself struggled to have peaceful and constructive conversations with my co-parent. Discussions about our daughter's well-being would often spiral into prolonged back-and-forth messaging, focusing solely on past hurts and actions. Ultimately, these exchanges would end without any resolution, other than not having contact for a few days. These relentless cycles of conflict are exhausting, and the subsequent stress symptoms would leave me drained, and less able to be a conscious and present parent. Feelings of guilt and regret can further complicate decision-making and boundary-setting during this time.

Anxiety and uncertainty can arise from concerns about parenting inadequacy or the fear of losing a bond with the children, which may lead to stress. I've observed this in my co-parent when our daughter expresses a desire to do something that falls outside the predictable plan.

To address these emotions, the first step is to acknowledge them and not push them away. These feelings are valid to have when worlds are turned upside down. Through this self-validation, co-parents can start embracing the fact that experiencing powerful emotions after a divorce or separation is common. Ultimately, this can support parents in moving forward.

Co-parents can connect with friends, take part in support groups, or seek therapy to express emotions and receive valuable advice when self-healing is not enough. To strive for peace and union is difficult in the face of intense emotions, where possible, shifting focus solely to the children's needs, can help parents unite on a different level.

Prioritising self-care significantly enhances resilience and the ability to manage co-parenting challenges. Engaging in self-care activities such as mindfulness, dancing, exercise, or journalling can help us regulate our emotional responses and reduce stress. Relationship breakdowns often serve as a catalyst for us to reflect on our behaviours and address deep-seated emotional wounds that contributed to the separation. Techniques like inner child exercises (to recognise and heal any childhood trauma) and shadow work (bringing the unconscious conscious) can be particularly illuminating when looking at unhealthy behavioural patterns. These methods delve into the psyche, helping individuals confront and integrate suppressed emotions and traumas, ultimately breaking patterns that once provided safety but are no longer needed.

By adopting these practices, co-parents can foster a healthier, more harmonious co-parenting relationship, benefiting both themselves and their children.

Despite emotional barriers, it is possible to create a positive co-parenting relationship. Setting emotional boundaries is essential to maintain a healthy connection and prevent personal problems from getting in the way. To maintain a professional co-parenting relationship, it's important to keep communication centred on the children and steer clear of triggers. Navigating their new roles requires co-parents to be patient with themselves and each other, allowing for emotional healing to take place.

Children who are sensitive and can be affected by tension and conflict can also be impacted by parents' emotions. By demonstrating healthy emotional management, we can teach children valuable skills for life. Cooperative co-parenting provides stability and security for children during a time of notable change. Effective emotional management by parents can cultivate a positive connection between children and both parents.

It is essential to understand the significance of personal responsibility in well-being and emotional management and the practical considerations involved in decision-making. You can use the following model when thinking about your own responsibility of choice when it comes to communicating through emotional barriers:

1. Persist in conflict: The first choice is to continue in a state of conflict or stress without seeking resolution or change. This choice involves accepting ongoing tension as a part of co-parenting. While it may seem like the path of least resistance, it carries risks, as prolonged conflict can negatively impact both the parents, and the children involved. Some individuals may feel they are gaining attention or sympathy from others due to their stressful situation, but this often comes at a high emotional cost.

2. Foster resilience: The second choice is to cultivate resilience within the co-parenting relationship. This means developing the ability to handle co-parenting challenges with a sense of strength and adaptability. Resilience might manifest as patience, clear communication, or the capacity to manage one's emotions during interactions with the other parent. It could also involve seeking support from friends, family, or professionals to navigate co-parenting more effectively.

3. Improve the co-parenting dynamic: The third choice involves actively working to change the co-parenting relationship for the better. This might mean setting clearer boundaries, establishing more structured communication protocols, or engaging in mediation or counselling to address underlying issues. By taking steps to improve the co-parenting dynamic, parents can create a more positive environment for themselves and their children.

4. Redefine boundaries or arrangements: The fourth choice is to make significant alterations to the co-parenting arrangement if the current situation proves unsustainable. This doesn't mean giving up on co-parenting, but rather reassessing and possibly restructuring the terms of engagement to better suit the well-being of all parties involved. This could involve legal modifications to child arrangement agreements or finding new ways to share responsibilities that reduce stress and conflict.

Overcoming emotional barriers is essential for co-parenting success. By recognising and dealing with emotions, seeking help, and prioritising your children's well-being, you can establish a nurturing environment that fosters emotional health and development. It's a path that calls for understanding, self-awareness and a resolve to move forward in the family's best interest.

Uncovering traumas that may affect co-parenting relationships is a delicate process that requires self-awareness, honesty, and often the guidance of a professional. Trauma can deeply influence how individuals react to stress, communicate, and manage conflict. Here is an approach that you can consider exploring to address any underlying traumas:

- **Self-reflection:** Begin with introspection. You can ask yourself questions about your past experiences, your reactions to certain co-parenting situations, and whether these reactions seem disproportionate to the event itself. Asking yourself questions about your past experiences can help you identify patterns that may be rooted in past trauma.

- **Journalling**: Keeping a journal to document thoughts, feelings, and reactions to co-parenting interactions can help you track triggers and identify potential links to past traumatic experiences.
- **Education**: Learning about trauma and its effects can provide you with the knowledge to recognise symptoms and patterns in your own behaviour that may be trauma-related.
- **Therapy**: Engaging with a therapist, especially one trained in trauma-informed care, can be instrumental in uncovering and addressing traumas. Therapists can use various techniques, such as cognitive behavioural therapy (CBT), eye movement desensitisation and reprocessing (EMDR), somatic experiencing, internal family systems (IFS), or even more radical approaches such as psychedelics to help individuals process and heal from trauma.
- **Trauma-specific assessments**: There are assessments and questionnaires designed to help identify trauma, such as the Adverse Childhood Experiences questionnaire. Therapists can use these tools in a therapeutic setting to help uncover traumas that may be affecting co-parenting.
- **Support groups**: Sometimes, sharing experiences with others who have similar challenges can help individuals recognise their own trauma. Support groups provide a safe space to explore these issues and learn from others.
- **Mind-body practices:** Techniques such as yoga, meditation and mindfulness can help individuals become more attuned to their bodies and recognise the physical manifestations of

trauma. This body awareness can be a gateway to understanding the emotional and psychological effects of trauma.

- **Couples or co-parenting counselling**: If both co-parents are willing, joint counselling sessions can help address how each individual's trauma affects their co-parenting relationship. A therapist can facilitate communication and provide tools for both parents to support each other in healing.
- **Trauma workshops and seminars**: Taking part in workshops and seminars focused on trauma can provide co-parents with insights into how trauma affects relationships and strategies for managing its impact.
- **Patience and compassion**: It's important for co-parents to approach this process with patience and compassion for themselves and each other. Uncovering and healing from trauma is a journey that takes time and effort.

It is key to remember that trauma recovery is a personal process, and what works for one individual may not work for another. It is important to seek out resources and support that resonate with you and to proceed at a pace that feels manageable. By addressing any traumas, you can work towards a healthier, more cooperative, co-parenting relationship that benefits both yourselves and your children.

CHAPTER 6: COMMUNICATION BREAKDOWNS AND BREAKTHROUGHS

So now we have understood a little more about the more emotional and physiological sides of why we may be reacting in certain ways. How do we apply this to our communication? This chapter will look at some of the pitfalls we can fall into with communicating, as well as strategies we can put in place for improvement.

The foundation of any successful co-parenting relationship is effective communication. Communication breakdowns often result in conflict and misunderstanding. Let's focus on understanding the causes of communication breakdowns and some strategies for achieving breakthroughs to enhance the co-parenting partnership.

The lingering feelings of hurt, anger or betrayal from the relationship can spill over into interactions during co-parenting. Without well-defined boundaries, conversations regarding children can devolve into personal attacks rather than productive discussions. External pressures, such as work stress, new relationships, or financial issues, can exacerbate these challenges, hindering effective communication and triggering painful past hurts.

Differences in parenting styles can also lead to conflict and miscommunication. Each of us tends to parent in a way that reflects our own upbringing and experiences. For me, this has been one of the most challenging aspects of co-parenting, and it remains a struggle. It's important to explain to children, in an age-appropriate way, that things might be done differently when they're with the other parent, and that's perfectly OK. Acknowledging and validating this for the children can help reduce their confusion. Accepting that we can't control what happens when they're with the other parent is key to finding peace with these differences. I used to try to control things to maintain consistency for my daughter, but as I've learned, trying to control only triggers stress in the other parent and leads to unproductive conversations. Letting go of the idea that we can influence what happens when our children are with the other parent is crucial for achieving our own inner zen.

The nuances of language are also key to acknowledge. The language we use with our co-parent and children can paint our experiences in different shades. Imagine two people from diverse backgrounds describing a family outing. One might focus on the laughter and joy, while the other remembers the stress of planning. This shows how our personal "language"—shaped by culture, emotions, and past experiences—can influence the way we perceive and remember different moments. Language doesn't just add colour to our stories; it can reshape our memories. Remembering this can also help tremendously in not taking everything that is relayed back through our children as the absolute truth.

As a quick exercise to establish any current communication traps that may be leading to conflict in the co-parenting relationship, parents can assess if, when and how often they are exhibiting the following:

- **Put-downs:** These include making negative or derogatory comments about each other.
- **Criticising:** Criticising your co-parent's parenting styles—this includes what the child does when with the other parent.
- **Removal of reminders of the child's other parent:** This includes removing pictures or anything that relates to your co-parent from your home. This can create confusion for the child. Remember, your children have two parents!
- **Blaming:** Blaming your co-parent for problems in your own life is avoiding personal responsibility and accountability—the only person who has control over you is you!
- **Quizzing:** This involves asking for excessive information about the other's life and what the child does on their time.
- **Not allowing your child to discuss the other parent:** If the child feels that it will upset you if they talk about their other parent, they will learn to censor what they say which affects their sense of safety and spontaneity. Your child loves both parents.

Understanding these factors is the initial phase in addressing and preventing communication breakdowns.

To convert communication challenges into opportunities for growth, co-parents can incorporate the following strategies:

- Demonstrating active listening involves truly hearing the other parent's perspective without interrupting or preparing to counter, which can result in increased empathy and understanding.
- When practising non-violent communication, the use of "I" statements and expressing needs and feelings without blame can decrease defensiveness and facilitate compromise.
- Scheduling regular check-ins can help avoid communication problems and keep issues from escalating.
- You may find that written communication, such as texts, emails or using a co-parenting app, aids in keeping interactions on track and preserving a record of agreements and decisions.
- If communication barriers become too overwhelming, professionals, such as therapists or co-parenting counsellors can offer guidance and improve dialogue.

Understanding how to communicate with your co-parent in a way that maximises what you need, but also respects the needs and opinions of others, will increase the likelihood of developing an effective and collaborative co-parenting relationship. Conflict arises as a result of differences between people. As seen, this can be amplified following divorce and separation as issues become mixed up with past hurts, emotions, and power struggles. Continuing conflict between co-parents can have a damaging effect on the ability of the children to adjust to their new circumstances and continue secure and loving relationships with both parents.

The Thomas-Kilmann Conflict Model (Fig 2) identifies five distinct conflict resolution styles: competing, accommodating, avoiding, collaborating, and compromising. Each style reflects a different level of assertiveness and cooperativeness in managing disputes:

- **Competing**: One parent insists on setting the rules without considering the other's views. This might resolve issues quickly but can lead to resentment and one-sided decision-making.
- **Accommodating**: A parent may consistently yield to the other's preferences to avoid conflict, which can lead to dissatisfaction and feeling undervalued or unheard.
- **Avoiding**: Parents may choose to ignore conflicts, leading to unresolved issues that could escalate into bigger problems affecting their children's stability.
- **Collaborating**: Ideal in co-parenting, it involves both parents working together to find solutions that consider and respect each other's needs and, most importantly, the best interests of the children.
- **Compromising**: This can be effective when collaboration is not possible. Both parents give up something to reach a mutually acceptable solution, ensuring that major decisions do not stall.

Using the model, co-parents can gain insight into their conflict resolution styles and adjust their approach to foster a more cooperative and harmonious relationship. By striving for a collaborative or compromising style, co-parents can ensure decisions are balanced and contribute positively to their children's upbringing.

Some case studies of breakthroughs

Sarah and John

Co-parents Sarah and John struggled to manage their children's schedules, often leading to frustration, and missed opportunities due to frequent miscommunications. They finally overcame this by using a shared online calendar. They decided on a platform that satisfied both and proceeded to enter all of their children's schedules into the calendar. This permitted both parents to monitor where and when the children needed to be, in real-time. Additionally, it allowed for the recording of essential event details like location and required equipment. As time passed, this system successfully diminished misunderstandings and ensured that both parents were fully informed, leading to improved well-being for their children.

Lisa and Mark

Co-parents Lisa and Mark had a difficult divorce that strained their personal relationship. Nevertheless, they both acknowledged the significance of creating a stable atmosphere for their children. They made an agreement to treat their co-parenting relationship as a business partnership, focusing on their children's welfare. They used email and text messaging to communicate professionally, always prioritising the children's needs. They established regular meetings, like those of business partners, to discuss upcoming decisions. They achieved effective joint decision-making by keeping personal grievances separate from their co-parenting responsibilities.

Mike and Emma

Mike and Emma's different parenting styles caused frequent disagreements on child-raising after their divorce, leading to joint counselling sessions for improved communication. To address their communication problems and how it was affecting their children, they made the decision to attend counselling sessions together. Through therapy, they concentrated on enhancing their communication skills, which involved learning to listen to one another and express concerns without turning them into arguments. In addition, the therapist guided them in recognising the value of presenting a united front to their children and equipped them with tools to navigate and reach agreements on parenting decisions. With time, they became more effective co-parents through these sessions and embraced teamwork to ensure their children's happiness and security.

Please note that all names have been changed for the purpose of this book. However, these real-life stories highlight that with the right tools, a commitment to the children's best interests and professional guidance when needed, co-parents can overcome communication barriers and create a positive environment for their children. Effective and respectful communication not only reduces the frequency and intensity of conflicts but also enables co-parents to make decisions that genuinely benefit their children. Ultimately, a cooperative co-parenting relationship enhances children's well-being by providing stability and a healthy communication model.

An additional point: it's important to acknowledge how easily human memory can be distorted in the realm of co-parenting. The questions co-parents ask each other can unknowingly guide their memories, sometimes causing them to diverge from what happened. This becomes particularly significant when settling conflicts or making decisions that depend on past incidents. Even with good intentions and believing in their own honesty, co-parents must acknowledge the possibility of incomplete or altered memories.

The communication dynamics among co-parents are greatly influenced by this phenomenon. One co-parent may unknowingly create misunderstandings or lead the other to misinterpret their intentions, subtly affecting their shared understanding.

It's essential for us to be mindful of the narratives we create and communicate. These narratives help simplify complex experiences but are often infused with personal interpretations. As a result, the mental image one co-parent holds may not fully align with the message the other is trying to convey.

To bridge these potential gaps between their viewpoints, co-parents are encouraged to ask targeted questions. Instead of posing a general question: "Have you handled the situation involving our child?" a more targeted question like, "How did you feel when you addressed our child's behaviour?" can offer deeper insight and a more enlightening perspective. By focusing on specifics, co-parents can build a more accurate and shared understanding, effectively navigating their shared responsibilities with greater clarity and empathy.

Co-parenting frequently involves communication challenges, but they can be resolved. By employing effective communication strategies and seeking professional assistance when needed, co-parents can make breakthroughs for a better co-parenting relationship. This leads to a positive atmosphere where their children can thrive and prosper.

Below are various tools and apps that can facilitate better communication, scheduling, and expense management for co-parents. These digital solutions can help reduce conflict and confusion by providing clear, centralised platforms for co-parents to coordinate their efforts.

Dedicated co-parenting apps

OurFamilyWizard

Features: Shared calendar, expense log, messaging, information bank and third-party access for family professionals.

Website: *www.ourfamilywizard.co.uk*

coParenter

Features: Co-parenting plans, mediation support, messaging with language filters and location check-ins.

Website: *www.coparenter.com*

2houses

Features: Calendar management, financial tracking, shared journal, and photo album.
Website: *www.2houses.com*

TalkingParents

Features: Secure messaging, shared calendar, and unalterable records for accountability.
Website: *www.talkingparents.com*

amicable

Features: Parenting plan support, expense tracking and a platform for amicable separation agreements.
Website: *www.amicable.io*

Messaging and scheduling tools

While not specifically designed for co-parenting, these general tools can be adapted for co-parenting communication:

WhatsApp

Features: Secure messaging and file sharing, useful for quick updates and sharing photos or documents.
Website: *www.whatsapp.com*

Google Calendar

Features: Shared calendars that can be used to track visitation schedules, appointments and school events.

Website: *www.calendar.google.com*

Conflict resolution platforms

For co-parents needing assistance with dispute resolution:

Peaceful Solutions

Features: Offers dispute resolution services to help co-parents resolve conflicts without going to court.
Website: *www.peacefulsolutions.org.uk*

myLawyer

Features: Connects co-parents with legal professionals for advice and mediation services.
Website: *www.mylawyer.co.uk*

Financial management tools

To help co-parents manage shared expenses:

Splitwise

Features: Tracks shared expenses and balances, making it easier to manage who owes what.
Website: *www.splitwise.com*

PayPal

Features: A secure way to transfer money between co-parents for child-related expenses.
Website: *www.paypal.com/uk/home*

Note: *It's important for co-parents to review the privacy policies and security features of any app or tool they choose to use, ensuring that their family's information is protected. Additionally, co-parents should agree on which tools they will use to avoid confusion and ensure consistent communication.*

As well as the practical solutions to communication clarity, self-assessment tools can be invaluable in identifying personal triggers and working towards more effective communication and collaboration. Here are some recommended tools and approaches that can help in this process:

- **Emotional journalling**: Keeping a journal to record instances of conflict and the emotions that arise can help you track patterns in your emotional responses. Over time, you may notice specific themes or situations that consistently trigger a strong reaction.
- **The Conflict Dynamics Profile**: This assessment tool helps individuals understand how they respond to conflict. It identifies constructive and destructive behaviours and can provide insight into how one's actions may escalate conflicts.
- **The Emotional Intelligence Appraisal**: Emotional intelligence (EI) is crucial for managing one's emotions and handling interpersonal relationships thoughtfully and empathetically.

This appraisal measures EI and can help you understand your emotional strengths and weaknesses.

- **The Trigger Point Analysis for co-parents**: This is a reflective exercise where you list out known triggers and analyse what about these situations causes a reaction. This can include time pressures, specific topics, or even particular words or phrases used during communication.

- **Mindfulness-based stress reduction programmes**: While not a self-assessment tool per se, these programmes can help you become more aware of your thoughts and feelings in the moment, which is a critical step in identifying triggers.

- **Online self-assessment quizzes**: There are numerous free online tools and quizzes designed to help individuals understand their reactions to stress and conflict. These can be a good starting point for co-parents to explore their triggers.

- **Professional psychological assessments**: Sometimes, working with a psychologist or licensed therapist to undergo a professional assessment can uncover deeper emotional triggers and issues. This can be particularly helpful if co-parents are dealing with unresolved issues from their relationship.

It's important for you to approach these tools with an open mind and a willingness to reflect honestly on your behaviours and emotions. The goal is not to assign blame, but to gain insight into our own patterns and behaviours, and work towards managing them more effectively for the sake of better co-parenting, and the well-being of the children.

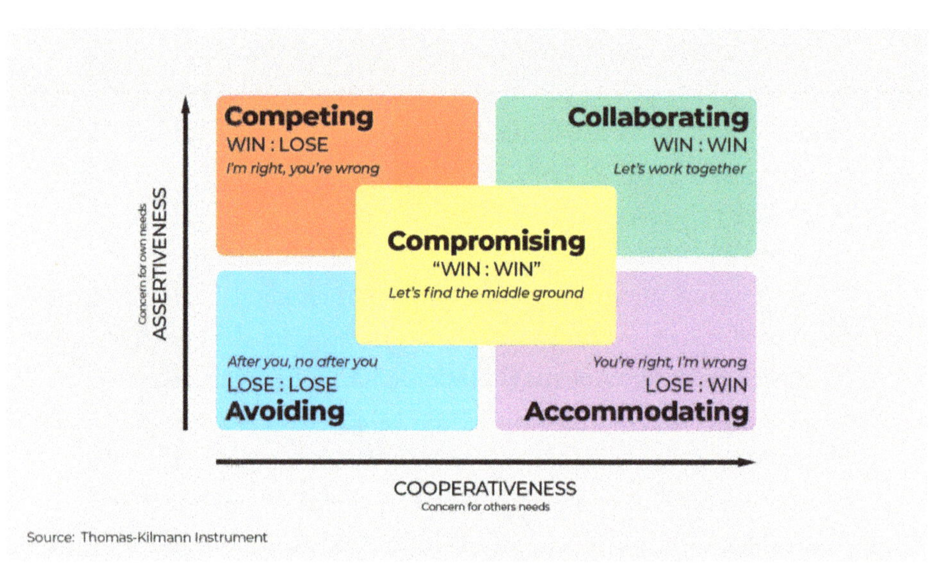

Fig 2: The Thomas Kilmann Conflict Model

CHAPTER 7: IF IT ALL GETS TOO MUCH—THE ROLE OF COUNSELLORS AND MEDIATORS

Sometimes, despite our best efforts, managing the complexities of co-parenting after a separation or divorce is too overwhelming. The involvement of professional counsellors and mediators can help facilitate a smoother transition for both parents and children.

The role of professional counsellors

Trained professional counsellors can provide support and guidance to individuals, couples and families experiencing significant life changes. When it comes to co-parenting, counsellors can aid parents in a variety of ways. As we have discussed, separation can elicit a variety of emotions, including anger, resentment, sadness, and grief. These feelings are important to address to co-parent effectively, and counsellors can help parents navigate them in a healthy manner. Successful co-parenting relies on effective communication. Counsellors can teach parents active listening, clear self-expression, and constructive dialogue.

Experts in child development and family dynamics can collaborate with parents to develop parenting plans that are optimal for the children. Counsellors can directly assist children in addressing their needs and adapting to changes in their family structure while providing a secure space for them to express their emotions.

The role of mediators

Acting as neutral intermediaries, mediators aid co-parents in negotiating and reaching agreements on distinct aspects of their parenting plan. Unlike counsellors, mediators concentrate on resolving disputes and discovering mutually satisfactory outcomes. Some ways that they can help are discussed below.

Mediators enable parents to engage in discussions about their issues in a structured setting, preventing conflicts from escalating. They advocate for fairness and uphold neutrality to guarantee equal participation for both parents in decisions regarding their children.

Mediators help guide parents towards agreements on contentious matters, such as access schedules, holidays, and financial obligations.

Finally, if required, mediators are often able to assist in the drafting of the necessary legal documents that solidify the co-parenting plan once an agreement has been reached.

Seeking assistance from professionals can promote a peaceful co-parenting relationship by mitigating conflicts.

They can guide parents to prioritise the needs of their children through child-centred solutions.

Compared to litigation, mediation offers a faster and more cost-effective way to reach agreements.

Long-term communication between co-parents can be significantly improved through the skills acquired in counselling and mediation, making the co-parenting process smoother. With the children's best interests in mind, they provide parents with the tools, support, and guidance necessary to navigate their new relationship dynamics effectively. Parents can use their expertise to establish a stable and cooperative co-parenting environment, promoting their children's healthy development.

When attempting to resolve conflict with an individual who is still working on their emotional maturity, if a co-parent's repeated attempts to raise something that they believe needs a conversation about is met with defensiveness, avoidance, criticism, or anger, then the involvement of a third party may be helpful. Honesty and vulnerability are essential for true connection and as co-parents, we are bringing up children together—arguably one of life's most important purposes. This may be enough of a reason to get in front of the professionals. As a reminder, your feelings are valid, you deserve respect and kindness as a baseline.

CHAPTER 8: THE IMPORTANCE OF FLEXIBILITY AND COMPROMISE

The dynamic nature of co-parenting requires both flexibility and compromise. In this chapter, we examine why these qualities are essential and how they can be incorporated into the co-parenting relationship to benefit both parents and children.

Co-parenting flexibility involves adapting to unforeseen circumstances and changes. Compromise is achieved when both parents are willing to negotiate on specific issues to find a solution, they can both accept.

Children's needs evolve as they grow, prompting parents to adapt their plans. Changes in jobs, relocations and other life events can require modifications to co-parenting arrangements. By adopting a flexible and compromise-oriented approach to co-parenting, the potential stress these events could bring is decreased.

Make the children a priority—when making decisions, always consider what is best for them, even if it means sacrificing personal preferences.

Regular, open communication allows co-parents to discuss changes and work together to find solutions. By including provisions for flexibility in the co-parenting plan, parents can better navigate future changes and work together towards finding solutions that are advantageous for both parents and children, rather than regarding compromises as losses.

Understanding the other parent's perspective through empathy can facilitate flexibility and finding common ground. Understanding the other parent's perspective through empathy means recognising they may have different wants and needs for the child. That's OK. The child's best interests come first. Any lingering animosity must be set aside. Only then can you acknowledge that you both share the same goal —raising a happy, healthy child. This realisation can lead to greater flexibility and cooperation.

Constructive co-parenting doesn't guarantee a peaceful, conflict-free relationship. It can be beneficial to embrace a healthy tension between differing perspectives, as this can lead to deeper insight and more balanced solutions. The notion that co-parenting can be reduced to black-and-white decisions is challenged. Instead, it is better understood as a spectrum of possibilities, each shaped by the complexities and nuances of family dynamics.

The ability to co-parent resiliently is not static, but rather a dynamic process of exploring, adapting, and growing. It entails consistently recalibrating our internal compasses to navigate the ever-evolving parenting difficulties. The main focus is on how personal choices impact resilience. At every crossroads, we have the opportunity to shape our behaviour and influence the co-parenting environment in ways that support not only the children's well-being but also our own.

From time to time, the interval between a provocation and the urge to respond swiftly is remarkably brief. In these fleeting moments, co-parents can prepare themselves and lay the foundation for making choices that align with their co-parenting goals. By doing so, they empower themselves to approach proposed changes with flexibility, compromise, and intention, fostering a resilient, adaptable co-parenting relationship that responds to the needs of the children.

For co-parents facing difficulties in reaching agreements, mediation is a valuable resource. Mediators can offer alternative solutions that parents might not have explored and can make sure discussions remain focused on the objective of finding viable solutions. They can also aid in negotiations, enabling parents to reach flexible and compromising agreements.

Embracing flexibility and compromise can result in an improved co-parenting relationship. When parents work together amicably, it sets a positive tone for their ongoing relationship.

Children experience improved outcomes when they are in a cooperative environment and are shielded from parental conflicts. A recent study finds that different types of positive childhood experiences (PCEs)—defined as having supportive relationships and nurturing environments—are strongly associated with improved mental and physical health in adulthood. The study, conducted by UCLA Health, suggests that these experiences might be especially protective against the effects of early life adversity. The research highlights that positive childhood experiences, such as feeling safe in the home, having at least one caregiver who genuinely listens, and participating in community traditions, are strongly linked to better mental and physical health outcomes in adulthood.

For co-parents, being flexible and willing to compromise can enhance personal growth and conflict-resolution abilities.

Flexibility and compromise are not signs of weakness but are indicative of a strong, child-focused co-parenting approach. Embracing these qualities enables us to establish a co-parenting relationship that is adaptable and harmonious, addressing the changing needs of our children and life circumstances. This approach supports the well-being of the entire family, cultivating a sense of unity and cooperation despite the obstacles of parenting in separate households.

CHAPTER 9: SETTING BOUNDARIES AND ESTABLISHING ROUTINES

To create a stable and healthy environment for children while co-parenting, it's essential to set boundaries and establish routines. In this chapter, we will explore the significance of these elements and offer practical advice on their successful implementation.

To begin with, it is worth discussing the different parenting styles that we all have. Parenting styles are generally categorised into four main types, each with its own approach to discipline, communication, and expectations. You can work out which is your current style by reviewing the following list:

Authoritative parenting: The child-centred approach

- **Characteristics**: Authoritative parents set clear rules and expectations but are also responsive and open to their children's needs. They enforce boundaries with reasoning and discussion with the children, encouraging independence while maintaining structure.

- **Communication**: Open, two-way communication where the child's opinions are valued.
- **Discipline**: Consistent and fair, with explanations for rules and consequences.
- **Outcome**: Children raised with authoritative parenting often develop strong social skills, high self-esteem, and a good sense of responsibility.

Authoritarian parenting

- **Characteristics**: Authoritarian parents have strict rules and elevated expectations, with little room for negotiation. They value obedience and discipline over flexibility and may be less responsive to the child's emotional needs.
- **Communication**: One-way communication, with the parent making decisions and expecting compliance.
- **Discipline**: Often harsh or punitive, with little explanation for the rules.
- **Outcome**: Children raised with authoritarian parenting may be obedient and proficient, but they might also struggle with low self-esteem, anxiety, or social skills.

Permissive parenting

- **Characteristics**: Permissive parents are indulgent and lenient, often avoiding confrontation. They have few demands or expectations and are highly responsive to their child's desires, sometimes to the point of allowing the child to make most decisions.

- **Communication**: Open and child-led, with the parent acting more like a friend than an authority figure.
- **Discipline**: Rarely enforced, with few rules and minimal structure.
- **Outcome**: Children raised with permissive parenting may struggle with self-discipline and authority, potentially leading to behavioural issues and difficulties with responsibility.

Uninvolved parenting (neglectful parenting)

- **Characteristics**: Uninvolved parents provide little guidance, nurturing or attention. They may be detached or indifferent to their child's needs, often due to stress, lack of knowledge or other personal issues.
- **Communication**: Minimal or non-existent, with little involvement in the child's life.
- **Discipline**: Lax or absent, with few rules or expectations.
- **Outcome**: Children raised with uninvolved parenting may experience a range of negative outcomes, including attachment issues, poor academic performance, and low self-esteem.

There are of course others that are used—helicopter, attachment, the list goes on. The child-centred approach I advocate in this book aligns closely with authoritative parenting, which emphasises a balanced blend of structure and responsiveness. In this style, we set clear expectations and boundaries while remaining attuned to our child's individual needs and perspectives. The child-centred approach promotes open communication, where the child's voice is valued, and their autonomy is respected. As parents, we act as guides rather than dictators, fostering an environment where our children feel secure, heard, and empowered. This approach encourages children to develop independence, self-discipline, and resilience, all within a supportive and nurturing framework that prioritises their well-being and personal growth.

In order to implement the approach, boundaries and routines with both children and the other co-parent are necessary. The establishment of boundaries in co-parenting clarifies the expectations and limits for parents' relationships with their children and each other. Each parent's time, space and parenting style are respected through clear boundaries and when these agreed-upon boundaries are respected, misunderstandings and disputes can be avoided. Perhaps most importantly, children's feelings of security and stability are strengthened when they have a clear understanding of what to expect from each parent. This ties into the strategy of being open and honest with children about the different experiences they may have with each parent and normalising them as much as possible. Of course, routine and structure, especially for younger children is key, however, we can't control what happens on the other side, all we can do is mitigate and support.

Guidelines for defining boundaries

Co-parents must have a conversation and establish mutual agreement on acceptable and unacceptable behaviour for both their interactions and their children's. When boundaries are unclear, they are more likely to be crossed, so being as precise as possible is key. By putting these boundaries in writing, you can include them in the co-parenting plan and avoid disagreements later on. It's also important for parents to ensure that these boundaries are appropriate for their child's age and comprehension. The key to effective boundaries is consistent maintenance and execution.

Establishing boundaries is essential for neural health, as it helps us balance stress and relaxation, which is crucial for optimal brain functioning. Neuroscience research has shown that chronic stress can alter the brain's structure and function, particularly in areas like the hippocampus, which is responsible for memory and emotional regulation. By setting boundaries, we reduce the risk of chronic stress, thereby protecting neural circuits. Additionally, boundaries support the production and regulation of neurotransmitters like serotonin and dopamine, which are vital for mood stabilisation and reward-based learning.

When we have clear boundaries, our brains can more effectively manage the influx of information, leading to improved focus, better decision-making and enhanced overall mental health. In essence, boundaries are not just psychological constructs—they have tangible effects on our brain's physiology, influencing both ourselves and our children's well-being. My own personal story meant that I put in place a firm boundary around talking about my co-parent's personal life. This helped me find my calm and inner peace when having conversations with him, and knowing our focus was on our child only. I no longer require this boundary having done the inner work required to better manage this, however, for the time it was in place, it was immeasurably helpful. Every time my co-parent attempted to break or cross the boundary, I could remind him of it and steer the conversation back to our child.

Example boundaries

- Respect each other's parenting time.
- Avoid negative talk about the other parent.
- Keep new relationships separate from the child.
- Encourage open parent-child conversation.

Helpful one-liners

- "Let's agree on specific times for handovers, so it's consistent and predictable for the children."
- "I think it's important we both have input on major decisions affecting the kids. Can we set up a time to talk about this?"
- "Let's try to keep our communication about the children focused and respectful, so we can both stay on the same page."

- "While I understand plans can change, could we try to give each other more notice if we need to alter the schedule?"
- "If we disagree, can we agree to take some time to think before responding, to keep our discussions constructive?"
- "I feel it's important for us to respect each other's personal space and time. Can we agree on what that looks like?"
- "Let's both make sure we're reinforcing the same rules and consequences with the children, so they have consistency from both homes."
- "Can we set up a protocol for how we handle emergencies with the children, so we're both prepared?"
- "I believe it's crucial we show respect in front of the children, even when we disagree. Can we commit to that?"
- OK, thanks for letting me know."
- "That's not true just because you said it."
- "That's not something I need to tell you."
- "OK, I hear you—what's your plan for that?"

The role of routines in co-parenting

The predictability and structure of routines are particularly comforting to children amidst family changes. They benefit from having daily schedules that include regular mealtimes, bedtimes, and homework routines. Maintaining consistent routines during pick-ups, drop-offs and transitions can also help decrease stress for both children and parents.

Last-minute conflicts can be avoided by having established routines for special events such as holidays and birthdays. As mentioned in Chapter 3, these occasions may trigger the emotions in the grief cycle and it's important for co-parents to honour these feelings and reach out for support where needed.

Collaborative scheduling is important for co-parents to consider the children's needs and the logistics of each parent's life. To be realistic, routines should be flexible and able to accommodate real-life situations. Co-parents can review and make necessary adjustments as children grow and circumstances change. By conducting regular reviews, routines can stay relevant and effective.

By following the established routines themselves, parents can model the consistency they expect from their children.

Setting boundaries and creating routines can be a complex process. Children may test boundaries and routines, especially during transitions. Stopping to understand *why* the child is behaving the way they are, and patience, is key. When co-parents clash over boundaries or routines, they may consider mediation or counselling to reach a middle ground.

It is also worth noting that established routines can be disrupted by changes in life circumstances like new jobs, relationships or moves. To manage these changes effectively, it is important to have flexibility and open communication.

Of course, this is not always possible. As children communicate their own wants and needs, it becomes more crucial than ever to ensure their voices are heard. Both parents must remain open-hearted and open-minded, giving their child a listening ear to truly understand what they need at that moment and act accordingly. Open communication is a must!

Establishing boundaries and routines is immeasurably helpful for a successful co-parenting relationship. They establish a framework that allows parents to operate with clarity and respect, while providing children with a stable and secure environment to thrive. Through careful implementation and maintenance of these structures, co-parents can foster a positive and supportive environment for their children's growth and development.

CHAPTER 10: BUILDING YOUR SUPPORT SYSTEM

In co-parenting, the importance of a solid support network outside of the legal arena cannot be overstated. In this chapter, we will discuss the significance of developing a support network that goes beyond legal help and courtrooms, providing practical guidance on building and sustaining this system to benefit parents and children.

The concept of the nuclear family, traditionally consisting of two parents and their children living in a single household, is increasingly considered outdated in the context of modern society's diverse and dynamic family structures. The challenges of today's world, such as co-parenting, have made it clear that relying solely on a nuclear family for raising children is not enough.

The phrase "it takes a village to raise a child" highlights the significance of a strong, community-like support system, especially in cases of separate households. By offering various perspectives, emotional support and practical assistance, these support systems contribute significantly to a child's development. Embracing this collective approach helps address the potential isolation and stress that single or separated parents encounter, promoting a powerful sense of community and belonging essential for both adults and children.

Co-parenting can be a challenging journey, and while legal professionals can help establish the framework for child arrangements and care, the day-to-day realities of raising children across two households require additional support. A well-rounded support system can provide emotional support to help manage the stress and emotional difficulties of co-parenting, as well as practical help with childcare, transportation, or busy schedules.

Co-parents are advised to consult experts or those who have faced similar situations for advice and guidance. An inclusive support system for co-parenting could consist of family and close friends—relatives and trusted friends who can offer emotional support, practical aid, and a compassionate presence. Single or co-parenting communities, known as parenting groups, provide a space for individuals to connect, share experiences and seek advice from others who can relate to their unique challenges. Therapists or counsellors specialising in family dynamics can offer valuable guidance for managing co-parenting challenges.

I strongly encourage you to enhance co-parenting and personal growth through educational resources like books, workshops, and seminars. Seeking support and advice is also made easier through online communities like forums and social media groups. When building a support system, don't be afraid to reach out for help from family and friends, or to seek out local or online support groups. Co-parents should choose supporters wisely, ensuring they are positive, understanding and genuinely interested in helping them succeed as co-parents.

The best support systems involve reciprocity and mutual support, so be prepared to lend a helping hand to others when the opportunity arises. Upholding boundaries is important for all of us to remember. Co-parents should ensure that their support system honours their co-parenting boundaries and respects the family's privacy. Regularly engaging in support groups and educational opportunities can offer ongoing benefits and help co-parents remain connected.

Of course, creating a support system has its own set of obstacles. Finding time to engage with support systems can be hard, but even short interactions can be helpful. While having support is vital, it's equally important for co-parents to foster their own coping strategies and decision-making skills to prevent overreliance.

Co-parents may also need to prepare for conflicting advice, as opinions may differ. It's important to consider what aligns with your individual family's needs and values. Having a staunch support system can greatly impact the co-parenting experience. Realising we are not alone in our co-parenting journey can alleviate the sense of isolation. With support, co-parents are better equipped to handle setbacks and challenges and increase resilience as a result. Broadening perspectives and accessing various resources can enhance parenting skills.

Establishing a support network beyond the legal realm can prove invaluable for successful co-parenting. With the support of family, friends, and community resources, co-parents can effectively raise children across two households. Not only does this network benefit parents, but it also creates a positive and stable environment for the children.

Books and literature

1. ***Mum and Dad Glue* by Kes Gray**: A child-friendly book that can help explain divorce and separation to young children.
2. ***Two Homes* by Claire Masurel**: A gently reassuring story focusing on what is gained, rather than what is lost, when parents divorce.
3. ***Family Breakdown: Helping Children Hang On To Both Their Parents* by Penelope Leach**: A guide to minimising the impact of separation on children.
4. ***The Unexpected Legacy of Divorce* by Julia M Lewis**: This book explains that while children do learn to cope with divorce, it in fact takes its greatest toll in adulthood, when the children of divorced parents embark on romantic relationships of their own.

Websites and online forums

1. **Gingerbread**: A charity supporting single-parent families that provides advice and forums for single parents (*www.gingerbread.org.uk*).
2. **The Parent Connection**: An online resource that offers advice on co-parenting after parting (*www.theparentconnection.org.uk*).

Professional services

1. **Family Mediation Council**: Find accredited family mediators who can help you resolve co-parenting disputes (*www.familymediationcouncil.org.uk*).
2. **Resolution**: A community of family justice professionals who promote a constructive approach to family disputes (*www.resolution.org.uk*).
3. **Relate**: Offers counselling services for every type of relationship nationwide (*www.relate.org.uk*).

Support groups

1. **OnlyMums & OnlyDads**: A national support service for parents who are going through or have gone through separation (*www.onlymums.org* and *www.onlydads.org*).

Educational workshops and seminars

1. **Parenting Apart workshops**: Run by Cafcass (Children and Family Court Advisory and Support Service), these workshops help parents understand separation from a child's perspective (*www.cafcass.gov.uk*).
2. **Family Lives**: Offers a range of services including parenting courses and family support (*www.familylives.org.uk*).

Additional resources

1. **Citizens Advice**: Provides free, confidential information and advice on legal, money and other problems (*www.citizensadvice.org.uk*).
2. **Child maintenance options**: Information and support on making child maintenance arrangements (*www.cmoptions.org*).

These resources can provide a starting point for co-parents seeking support and guidance. Whether you're looking for professional services, peer support or educational material, these resources can help you navigate the challenges and opportunities of co-parenting.

CHAPTER 11: BRINGING IT ALL TOGETHER WITH A CO-PARENTING PLAN

Now that we've covered some of the practical points to keep in mind, what's next? Creating a co-parenting plan can be incredibly valuable as we navigate the transition from a shared household to separate lives, while continuing to raise our children together. By developing a well-considered co-parenting plan, parents can establish a stable and predictable setting for their children and minimise conflicts.

It's important to remember that the plan is an opportunity to prioritise the child's needs over the co-parent's differences.

A co-parenting plan establishes the guidelines for parents to navigate childrearing after a separation or divorce. It's an in-depth agreement that addresses various aspects of parenting such as:

- Child arrangements and visitation schedules.
- School holiday arrangements.
- Communication methods and frequency.
- Decision-making processes for education, healthcare, and other important matters.
- Financial responsibilities, such as child support and expenses.

- How new partners will be integrated.
- Transportation and exchange coordination.

The main purpose of the plan is to ensure the children's needs are taken care of and that both parents have a clear understanding of their roles and responsibilities.

Steps to developing a co-parenting plan

Before creating a plan, it's important to evaluate the age, temperament, and requirements of each child. More transitions between homes may be necessary for younger children, whereas older children might find longer stays with each parent beneficial.

Parents should encourage open and honest communication regarding expectations and concerns. This is the time to have a conversation about work schedules, living arrangements and the children's activities to establish a realistic and achievable plan.

Using a template or seeking advice from a mediator or legal professional can be beneficial in preventing misunderstandings by including all necessary details.

The plan should strike a balance between being comprehensive and allowing for flexibility. Adjustments may be necessary to the plan as children grow and life circumstances shift. Regular plan reviews enable parents to make necessary updates.

Throughout the process, the focus should be on the best interests of the children. It's key to base decisions on what will aid their growth, development, and emotional well-being.

Creating a co-parenting plan can be challenging. Parents may disagree or find it tough to handle the emotional aspects of their separation. To help with this, it can be useful to work with a professional mediator or counsellor. This neutral third party can guide conversations and help parents reach an agreement, always keeping the child's best interests in mind.

When we're stressed, our ability to think clearly, focus, remember details and respond quickly can suffer. However, research shows that our brains can keep learning and adapting throughout life, which means co-parents can always improve how they plan, work together, and support their children.

To do this well, co-parents should approach challenges with the curiosity and creativity that children naturally have. Sir Ken Robinson, a well-known education advisor, pointed out that children aren't afraid to make mistakes and take risks. In contrast, adults often become afraid of being wrong, which can hold back creativity and make co-parenting planning more difficult.

When co-parents don't challenge themselves to think differently, their brains can become less motivated to learn new skills. For example, if one co-parent relies too much on the other's strengths, they might miss the chance to contribute more effectively.

This can weaken personal resilience and lead to unhealthy habits where co-parents rely too much on others or feel helpless. To make the most of their ability to adapt, co-parents should regularly rethink their plans as their child grows. Some changes in co-parenting strategies might happen quickly, while others might take time and practice.

For a co-parenting plan to work well, cooperation, communication and a focus on the children's well-being are essential. By embracing change and working together, parents can create a stable, caring environment where their children can thrive, even with unexpected changes in the family.

Below is a sample template and example of a co-parenting plan and agreement that can be adapted to fit specific needs. These samples are designed to help you create a structured and comprehensive approach to co-parenting.

Sample co-parenting plan

A co-parenting plan is a detailed agreement created by co-parents outlining how they will raise their children following separation or divorce. Here is an outline for a basic co-parenting plan:

1. **Introduction**

- Names of parents.
- Names and ages of children.
- Statement of mutual commitment to the children's well-being.

2. **Residence and contact schedule**

- Primary residence for the children.

- Regular contact schedule (weekdays, weekends).
- Holiday arrangements.
- Special occasions (birthdays, religious events).

3. Education and extracurricular activities

- Choice of school and educational decisions.
- Involvement in parent-teacher meetings.
- Participation in extracurricular activities.

4. Healthcare

- Medical, dental, and mental health arrangements.
- Emergency medical decisions.

5. Communication

- Methods and frequency of communication between co-parents.
- Guidelines for communication with the children when with the other parent.

6. Decision-making

- Process for making major decisions affecting the children.
- Day-to-day decision-making responsibilities.

7. Financial support

- Child support arrangements.
- Division of costs for education, healthcare, and extracurricular activities.

8. Transportation and exchange

- Coordination of transporting children between homes.
- Exchange locations and times.

9. Conflict resolution

- Agreed method for resolving disputes (e.g. mediation).

10. Review and modification

- Schedule for reviewing the co-parenting plan.
- Process for making modifications.

Sample agreements

In addition to the comprehensive co-parenting plan, co-parents may need to draft specific agreements for certain situations. Here are examples of clauses that might be included:

- **School holiday schedule agreement**: A detailed schedule for where the children will spend each school holiday, alternating arrangements each year if necessary.
- **Education agreement**: An agreement on the choice of schools, handling of educational expenses, and attendance at school-related events.
- **Medical care agreement**: A plan for making decisions about the children's medical care.

Checklists

To ensure all important aspects are covered, co-parents can use the following checklists when drafting their plans and agreements:

- **Residence and contact checklist**: Addresses living arrangements, visitation schedules and special dates.
- **Education checklist**: Covers school enrolment, academic support, and parent involvement.
- **Healthcare checklist**: Includes medical decision-making and emergency protocols.
- **Financial support checklist**: Outlines child support, additional expenses, and financial record-keeping.

These sample plans, agreements and checklists are intended to serve as a starting point. Co-parents should tailor these documents to their family's unique needs and, where necessary, seek legal advice to ensure their agreements are enforceable and in line with appropriate family law.

CHAPTER 12: LEGAL VS NON-LEGAL SOLUTIONS IN CO-PARENTING CONFLICT

Understanding your legal rights is of utmost importance in co-parenting. The rights differ based on factors like marital status, child agreements, court orders and country laws. It's important to delve into the legal rights that co-parents should be familiar with. Note this content is correct as of 2024.

Parental Responsibility

This is the legal term for the rights, duties, powers, responsibilities, and authority that a parent has for a child and the child's property. Mothers automatically have parental responsibility. Fathers also have parental responsibility if they are married to the mother at the time of the child's birth or have acquired it through a Parental Responsibility Agreement, by being listed on the birth certificate (for births registered from December 1, 2003), or by a court order.

Residence Orders

A residence order decides where a child will live. This can be granted to one parent or shared between both, which is sometimes referred to as shared parenting.

Contact Orders

These orders determine how the parent who is not living with the child will have contact with them. This can include visiting the child, the child staying with the parent, or indirect contact such as phone calls.

Specific Issue Orders

These are orders to resolve a particular issue in dispute in relation to a child, such as which school they should attend or whether they should receive a particular type of medical treatment.

Prohibited Steps Orders

These orders prevent a parent from making certain decisions about a child's life, such as taking them out of the country, without the consent of the court or the other parent with parental responsibility.

Child Arrangement Orders

Introduced in April 2014, these orders replace residence and contact orders. They can regulate arrangements relating to with whom a child is to live, spend time, or otherwise have contact with, and when these arrangements are to take place.

When co-parents cannot agree on these details, they have assorted options available to them when faced with these conflicts. In this chapter, we examine diverse ways to resolve disputes, comparing legal solutions (courts and the legal system) with non-legal options like mediation and collaborative practice. Co-parents can make informed decisions by understanding the strengths and limitations of each approach, which will best suit their family's needs.

The legal system offers a structured approach to resolving co-parenting conflicts. Usually, this entails dealing with solicitors and potentially going through legal proceedings. Key factors of legal solutions cover legally binding decisions and safeguarding. Courts can enforce legally binding decisions on child arrangements, financial support and other parental concerns and also safeguard the rights of both parents and children. However, legal remedies can present certain downsides as well. Legal proceedings can be costly, with expenses arising from solicitor fees, court fees and potential barrister representation. I have a friend who has spent over quarter of a million pounds in court proceedings spanning 2 years—remember, the private law system makes money through conflict.

Going through the courts to resolve conflicts can take a long time, causing prolonged stress and uncertainty for the family. Court battles can also worsen tensions and harm co-parenting relationships due to their adversarial nature. Further, children's preferences are disregarded in legal agreements, often prioritising the desires of adults.

The Family Forum is a group of parents, carers, and extended family members with direct experience in private law or public law proceedings. Cafcass established this group in September 2021 to listen to adults with experience in proceedings and to use their feedback to improve its work. The top tips below are based on the experiences of Family Forum members, who have devised them to help separating parents think about how they can minimise the damaging effects of separation and court proceedings on their children.

- Court proceedings should be the last resort. Court can be expensive, and you may not get the desired outcome. Think of other ways to resolve the issues, such as mediation, before going to court.
- Court proceedings can take a long time, and the length of time can damage your child's emotional well-being and their relationship with both parents.
- If your child is struggling emotionally, speak to professionals and seek support from their school or GP.
- The court process is traumatic for everyone involved. Remember to take care of your own well-being during this

process.

- When both parents have good communication with one another, the child can see that they have their best interests at heart.
- Both parents love their child and want the best for them. Arguing and criticising each other in front of your child may make them think otherwise.
- Avoid sharing your current difficulties on social media as your child may become aware, causing them upset and embarrassment.
- Please encourage and support your child's relationship with all of their grandparents and other family members. They love your child too and want to maintain a relationship with them.

(These guidelines are from February 2023 and are a stark reminder of the enormity of using the court as a tool to settle disagreements over children.)

The emphasis of the non-legal solutions outlined below lies in collaborating and negotiating outside of the courtroom.

- Co-parents can use mediation as a way to have productive discussions and find a mutually acceptable agreement. It is common to encourage mediation prior to resorting to court.
- In collaborative practice, each parent hires a collaboratively trained solicitor and commits to resolving issues without involving the court.
- Family arbitration involves an arbitrator who has the power to make a decision on the dispute, which is legally binding and resolved outside of the court system. The Institute of Family

Law Arbitrators (IFLA) runs the family arbitration scheme, which is known as the "Family Law Arbitration Scheme."

- Family counselling and therapy can help parents understand and manage their feelings about the separation and learn how to better communicate with each other for the sake of their children.

The benefits of the non-legal route are substantial. Generally, these methods are more affordable than taking legal action and rather than waiting for a court date, solutions can be reached quickly. Above all, these non-legal measures encourage cooperation and communication which helps maintain and strengthen co-parenting relationships.

Of course, the non-legal route also has its challenges. Agreements that are not made into court orders may lack legal enforceability. Both parents need to be willing to participate and compromise voluntarily, but this may not be possible in every situation. Legal intervention may be necessary for resolving certain issues that are too complex or contentious.

There are several variables that co-parents can use when deciding which path to take. It's important for co-parents to consider these factors when deciding between legal and non-legal solutions:

- Does the conflict necessitate legal intervention to protect the rights of the child or parents, or is it something that can be resolved through negotiation?
- Are the co-parents capable of effective communication or is the strained relationship an obstacle to collaboration?

- Which approach is in the child's best interests for their well-being?

When conflicts arise, co-parents have a variety of options to choose from. Resolving disputes through legal means is formal and binding, but it can be expensive and hostile. Both parties must be willing to engage in the process for non-legal solutions to be effective and cost-efficient. Through careful consideration of the pros and cons, co-parents can decide on the best course of action for their family.

In an article on *Psychology Today* entitled "Co-Parenting and High Conflict," Edward Kruk PhD states that "interparental conflict increases in sole custody arrangements and decreases over time in shared parenting arrangements; when neither parent is threatened by the loss of his or her children, conflict goes down." This is worth remembering as we push for the child-centred approach.

PART II: FEELING SAFE AGAIN

As we navigate the often-turbulent waters of raising children between two homes, the journey can be fraught with challenges and learning experiences. In Part II, I offer guidance to co-parents, promoting understanding, growth, and positive reinforcement. This is the place where the tumultuous past gives rise to a peaceful future, offering parents and children the assurance, steadiness, and potential for growth.

In this section, we explore the transformative power of introspection, the strength that comes from embracing personal development and the profound impact of fostering a nurturing co-parenting relationship. Each chapter provides insights and practical strategies for co-parents to turn past difficulties into valuable lessons, reinforce positive dynamics within their unique family structures, and cultivate an environment where everyone can flourish.

CHAPTER 13: LEARNING AND GROWING FROM PAST MISTAKES

The journey of co-parenting is seldom easy. Along the way, parents are bound to encounter obstacles and make mistakes. However, if co-parents approach these mistakes with introspection and a desire to learn, they can serve as powerful drivers for growth and beneficial changes. We explore the constructive process of learning from past mistakes in the following chapter.

Admitting past mistakes is the initial step in the process of learning from them. Acknowledging where we went wrong can be challenging, requiring honesty and humility with ourselves and our co-parent. It is essential to acknowledge these mistakes to progress, whether they were a result of miscommunication, unfulfilled promises or acting based on emotions.

Once mistakes are recognised, it's necessary to grasp how they affect children, the co-parenting dynamic and oneself. Co-parents are invited to contemplate how these actions might have influenced trust, stability, and the emotional well-being of those involved. Having this understanding can prevent making the same mistakes again.

Forgiveness plays a crucial role in the process of learning from past mistakes. It includes forgiving oneself for mistakes and, if necessary, asking for forgiveness from the co-parent and children. It's just as important for one parent to offer forgiveness to the other parent for their mistakes, as it promotes understanding and cooperation.

So many people struggle to find joy in their lives because they can be stuck in the past. Or they believe that forgiveness is something done for others to absolve them of the hurt they have caused. Forgiving ourselves is equally, if not more, important as a tool for self-healing.

Any traumatic memories that linger from the relationship and are triggered during conversations can often hinder the process of forgiveness. The ancient Greek saying 'know thyself' highlights the importance of recognising one's own strengths and weaknesses as a co-parent.

The ability to manage emotional responses can be greatly impacted by transforming intense memories into less vivid sketches, resulting in a profound change in perspective. For co-parents encountering challenges, this technique can be highly valuable.

The opportunity to implement lessons learned arises through acknowledgement and forgiveness. This may involve improving communication and committing to openness, honesty, and respectful exchanges with the other co-parent.

Making a conscious effort to alter behaviours that have led to previous errors can also help. Co-parents can keep in mind that the most effective apology is a shift in actions. Well-defined boundaries can help avoid future conflicts and misunderstandings, supporting co-parents as they develop plans for handling stressful situations or disagreements more constructively.

Support from others can greatly enhance the effectiveness of learning from past mistakes. Parents can seek guidance, perspective and encouragement from friends, family, therapists, or co-parenting counsellors from their support systems to improve their co-parenting relationship.

Neuroscience provides valuable insights into cognitive processes that can be useful in co-parenting. Regulating breathing and heart rate are techniques that parents can use to stay composed in stressful situations.

Moving forward with confidence is possible! By learning from our mistakes, we can become more confident in our parenting and decision-making abilities. Continuous learning and adaptation benefit us and teach our children that growth is possible after setbacks.

It's important to emphasise that mistakes are not the end of the road but rather stepping stones to a more effective and harmonious co-parenting relationship. By embracing growth and learning from the past, we can build a resilient foundation for our children's future.

Nurturing a child's growth relies heavily on developing self-awareness. It is easy to blame external people and circumstances. The real challenge and catalyst for transformation lies in going inside the heart and mind, understanding how and why certain triggers provoke such strong responses, and then working with them to gain understanding, rather than against them out of fear.

CHAPTER 14: THE POWER OF POSITIVE REINFORCEMENT

Employing positive reinforcement as a strategy can transform co-parenting, encouraging positive behaviours and strengthening the parent-child connection. In this chapter, we will explore the benefits of incorporating positive reinforcement into the co-parenting framework to create a more supportive family environment.

Encouraging and rewarding positive conduct in co-parenting employs the concept of positive reinforcement, increasing the probability of the repetition of the desired behaviour.

In co-parenting scenarios, it can serve various purposes to promote a culture of respectful conduct. Some are outlined below:

- Encourage cooperative behaviour and enhance problem-solving skills.
- Motivate children to adapt to changes in co-parenting schedules and transitions.
- Encourage both children and parents to build self-esteem and experience a sense of achievement.

So, how to do it? A little verbal praise can make a substantial difference, like saying "I appreciate how flexible you are" or "You handled that situation really well." Always be mindful to not undermine this strategy by sounding patronising—authenticity is powerful!

Co-parents can reinforce positive interactions by spending quality time with children or arranging a co-parenting meeting in a pleasant location. This may seem completely unworkable for some, but again, focusing on the joy it may bring to the child, rather than the pain and hurt between co-parents, is always a more helpful perspective.

Children who adapt to changes or show maturity in challenging situations can benefit from small rewards or incentives. Rewarding children for good behaviour, rather than punishing them for bad, can be one of the most effective behaviour modification techniques that parents can use.

Giving credit for the effort in co-parenting, regardless of the result, motivates ongoing collaboration. By focusing on positive behaviours, conflict and mistakes can be greatly reduced. In combination with open and constructive communication through positive feedback, this consistent positive reinforcement can aid in rebuilding trust between co-parents. While positive reinforcement is effective, it must be used correctly. Inconsistent reinforcement can lead to confusion in children and diminish its effectiveness.

Authenticity is key when giving praise and rewards, ensuring they reflect genuine achievements or efforts. Positive reinforcement should not be employed as a means of manipulating or controlling the other parent or children. As mentioned above, positive reinforcement in co-parenting is particularly advantageous for children, as it encourages them to repeat good behaviours and promotes their understanding of cooperation and respect.

When children witness their parents working together in a positive manner, they experience a greater sense of emotional security.

When parents use positive reinforcement, they serve as role models for healthy interaction and acknowledgement of others' contributions.

The co-parenting relationship can undergo a transformative change with the power of positive reinforcement. Creating a nurturing environment for children involves co-parents focusing on the positive and rewarding good behaviours, fostering growth, cooperation, and mutual respect. This approach benefits both the children and strengthens the co-parenting bond, promoting a more harmonious family dynamic.

CHAPTER 15: EMBRACING PERSONAL GROWTH FOR BOTH PARENTS

The co-parenting journey involves more than just the relationship with the other parent and caring for the children. This chapter looks at how co-parents can enrich their lives and strengthen their co-parenting bond through personal growth.

Self-improvement and self-discovery are key components of personal growth, leading to a more fulfilling life. It can help us to develop better emotional resilience and coping strategies and discover a greater sense of self-awareness and emotional intelligence. This can then result in better communication and conflict-resolution capabilities. Perhaps most importantly, this journey of self-discovery will promote overall happiness and well-being, which ultimately helps our children.

My own journey of transformation began in 2016 when I travelled to Costa Rica and spent three weeks alone, experiencing the healing and transformative effects of plant medicine. This experience provided me with the clarity and strength to end my marriage, after years of struggling with infidelity and fertility challenges.

I then, soon after, began my parenting adventure. Parenting undoubtedly forces us all to face some of our deep-seated wounding, as we get triggered and react in unhelpful ways to our children, often based on our own unhealed hurts and past modelling of family dynamics. There is a saying that the fastest path to enlightenment is to become a parent—I fully concur. When I became a mother in an emotionally uncertain world, I was deeply rooted in survival mode, and my sympathetic nervous system's freeze response took over. I can now recognise this and better understand some of my reactions and responses in certain situations. When I was thrust into co-parenting, I had no choice but to stand up and keep moving forward for the sake of my daughter. I was constantly triggered and overwhelmed by my co-parent and felt utterly helpless and abandoned. I struggled with the hurt and confusion I witnessed in my daughter, as well as my own heartbreak. This is why I have authored this book; I can empathise and sympathise with co-parents who find themselves in these seemingly impossible situations. It was one of the darkest times in my life. And of course, we have children to raise during this whole time—nobody can prepare us for this divided world where children are confused, co-parents are confused, and nobody has a clear rulebook. I decided to stop looking externally and blaming everything on my co-parent or life in general, he was doing his best, given the circumstances at the time.

As part of my own healing, I dedicated myself to self-improvement, learning about everything I write here in this book and feeling fascinated by my discoveries. I spent the time I was without my daughter, no longer in "freeze" state, but seeing friends, going out dancing, reading, learning new skills, and finding my joy again.

My experience with psychedelic therapy in 2023 solidified my understanding of my self-transformation. It helped me uncover suppressed trauma and unhelpful behavioural patterns that had shaped my life up until that point. While we are always learning and developing a deeper understanding of ourselves, this particular experience was enlightening. It marked a significant step forward in how I now approach co-parenting, as well as life in general.

Of course, everyone has their own beliefs and structures in which they operate, and all journeys are different. I have been in despair, not wanting to continue and helplessly watching my sweet child struggling with confusion and sadness. I know firsthand how debilitating it can be and want to emphasise that you are not alone. There is hope and light at the end of that tunnel. The resilience and power that is built through facing our deepest fears and choosing love and peace, over conflict and adversity, is truly life-changing. We attract what we are, not what we want. The more work, love and support we give ourselves; the more miracles will happen, and the better experience our children get from our parenting.

It must be acknowledged that some co-parents are in situations where they cannot safely be in proximity of the other. In these scenarios, this book will hopefully help individuals implement the strategies and guidance for themselves and still see the benefits.

Some of the methods that co-parents may wish to concentrate on for cultivating personal development could be:

- Engaging in therapy, meditation, journalling, and inner trauma work to process emotions linked not just to the relationship's conclusion, but also to childhood experiences that affect co-parenting challenges.
- By prioritising exercise, nutrition and rest, physical well-being can be enhanced, resulting in improved mood and energy levels. The more rest and sleep we have, the more able our brains are to cope with the episodes of stress that can occur throughout daily life. A bio-energetic nutrition protocol can give co-parents the necessary health and energy required to live through intense stress. Dr Ray Peat's ideas have revolutionised my approach to health. This was what helped turn around my fertility issues in 2017, and I now adopt the lifestyle promoted through this approach as a matter of course.
- Pursuing educational opportunities, reading, and learning new skills can foster intellectual development, self-discovery, and a sense of fulfilment.
- Social connections involve developing and sustaining friendships and social networks to offer support and alleviate loneliness. I cannot thank my support network enough for the love and care they have provided throughout my own co-parenting experience.
- Journeying into the spiritual realm and exploring practices and beliefs that bring comfort, purpose, and connection, such as energy healing, sound frequency, and other lesser-known methods.

The idea of dedicating time and effort to individual growth, rather than distracting activities such as housework, laundry, etc. can seem scary and overwhelming to those who are in challenged nervous system states. Co-parents may feel exhausted and numb, and this can lead to complacency. Having the courage to look at ourselves honestly can be utterly terrifying for our egos. It is important to remain compassionate to yourselves and keep the faith. It is not an easy journey, but the results make it all worthwhile. It is sometimes helpful to set goals, making these goals realistic and achievable based on the current state of central nervous system functioning.

Setting dedicated time aside on a consistent basis will help reprogramme the brain for success. Even as little as 10 minutes in the morning for some grounding by standing barefoot on the grass, meditating, or listening to some sound frequency healing, can go a long way towards healing burnt-out and frazzled systems. It's a marathon, not a sprint!

Connect with others for support by joining groups or finding mentors who can offer guidance and encouragement. As discussed in Chapter 10, the benefits of a strong support system are priceless. Even if that support system is one other person, let yourselves be supported!

Spending time in green spaces or bringing nature into everyday life can benefit mental and physical well-being. It can improve mood, reduce feelings of stress or anger, and make us feel more relaxed. It's possible to still get these positive effects from nature while staying indoors at home. You can spend time with the windows open to let in fresh air.

Arrange a comfortable space to sit, perhaps by a window with a view of trees, the sky, or birds and other animals. Listen to natural sounds, either from recordings or apps that play birdsong, ocean waves, or rainfall. Get as much natural light as possible. Spend time in your garden, if you have one, or open your front or back door.

Just as with children and the other co-parent, positive reinforcement is key when working on ourselves. Regularly reflecting on improvements, modifying goals accordingly, and embracing progress are essential. Acknowledge and celebrate important milestones in your personal development—this is your life to take control of and make the best it can be for both you and your children.

It's important to balance personal growth with co-parenting responsibilities. When the opportunity arises, consider enhancing the co-parenting relationship by applying new skills and insights. Sharing positive changes with your co-parent can encourage their own development, as we often mirror each other's growth. The more personal development you pursue, the more you may see it reflected in your co-parent.

Keep personal development consistent with your children's routines to ensure their stability. When co-parents focus on personal growth, it can positively impact the co-parenting relationship through new perspectives and improved skills. Increased self-awareness and understanding of behavioural patterns can lead to reduced conflicts, and children benefit from observing their parents actively pursuing lifelong learning and self-improvement.

Investing in personal development not only improves your life but also fosters a more cooperative and empathetic co-parenting dynamic. Embracing personal growth is a gift for yourself, the co-parenting partnership and the children who are influenced by their parents.

However, it's important to remain flexible as a parent, even in the midst of self-discovery. Recognising that behaviours and self-identity can evolve—much like changing clothes for different occasions or roles—is crucial. I found the book *The Inner Work* by Matthew Micheletti and Ashley Cottrell to be a helpful stepping stone in getting started.

As beautifully put by Carl Jung, "Your vision will become clear only when you can look into your own heart. Who looks outside, dreams, who looks inside, awakes." Self-care is an essential, yet often overlooked, aspect of single parenting and co-parenting. Below are some practical self-care tips to help single parents maintain their well-being, which is crucial for their own health and for their ability to effectively care for their children.

Physical self-care

1. **Regular exercise**: Incorporate physical activity into your routine, whether it's a gym session, a jog in the park, a yoga class or maybe just a decision to walk to and from the school for drop-offs and pick-ups. Exercise can improve mood and reduce stress. I find that going out and dancing all night is an excellent regulation technique and really helps me to let go,

recalibrate and de-stress. Me and my daughter also have regular kitchen dance parties to ensure we are both regulated and stress-free.

2. **Nutritious diet**: Eating a balanced diet can boost energy levels and overall health. Plan meals ahead to make healthy eating more convenient.

3. **Adequate sleep**: Prioritise getting enough sleep. Establish a bedtime routine and create a comfortable sleep environment to improve sleep quality. I find a 15-minute sound frequency healing before bed helps my sleep hugely.

Emotional self-care

1. **Mindfulness and relaxation**: Practice mindfulness, meditation, or deep-breathing exercises to manage stress and stay grounded.

2. **Journalling**: Keep a journal to express thoughts and feelings. Writing can be a therapeutic way to process emotions and gain clarity.

3. **Music therapy:** Studies are finding a growing body of evidence supporting the beneficial effects of music therapy, not only for adults but also for children and adolescents, in improving well-being and quality of life.

4. **Seek support**: Don't hesitate to reach out to friends, family, or support groups when you need to talk or seek advice.

Social self-care

1. **Maintain social connections**: Make time to maintain friendships and socialise. Adult interaction is important for emotional support and can provide a break from parenting duties. This was one of the positives that I eventually saw following my initial resistance to co-parenting. The time that my daughter spends with her dad gives me an opportunity to have quality time for myself. Whether being with friends or taking the time to be alone and happy in my own company.
2. **Join support groups**: Connect with other single parents through local or online support groups where you can share experiences and advice.

Intellectual self-care

1. **Pursue interests**: Engage in hobbies or interests that stimulate your mind and bring you joy.
2. **Continued learning**: Consider taking courses or attending workshops that interest you or contribute to your personal and professional development.

Spiritual self-care

1. **Reflection**: Spend time in reflection or prayer if it aligns with your beliefs. This can provide a sense of peace and purpose.
2. **Nature**: Spend time outdoors. Connecting with nature can be calming and rejuvenating.
3. **Energy Healing:** I personally chose to dedicate time to becoming a qualified energy healer in order to better manage challenging situations and dynamics. If this is of interest, you

can check out: One Light Healing Touch (OLHT):
www.onelighthealingtouch.com

Practical self-care

1. **Time management**: Use planners or apps to manage your time effectively. Prioritise tasks and learn to say no when necessary.
2. **Financial planning**: Keep on top of your finances with budgeting tools or advice from financial counsellors to reduce money-related stress.
3. **Delegate and ask for help**: Remember that it's OK to ask for help from family and friends, whether it's for childcare, errands, or household tasks.

Self-care is not selfish—it's a necessary part of being a good parent. By taking care of your own needs, you ensure that you have the physical energy, mental clarity, and emotional stability to be fully present and engaged in your children's lives. Remember to treat self-care as a priority, not a luxury, and find strategies that work best for you and your unique circumstances.

CHAPTER 16: HOW OUR OWN CHILDHOODS INFLUENCE OUR PARENTING

In order to begin to think about our own behaviours in relationships, as well as those of our children, an understanding of attachment theory can be helpful. Here I will briefly discuss some of the overarching principles.

In simple terms, Jonathan Bowlby describes his theory of attachment as a "lasting psychological connectedness between human beings." His theory suggests that strong emotional bonds are crucial for relationships. He observed that these bonds are shown through specific behaviours and motivations like children seeking comfort from their main caregiver when scared.

The attachment theory explains how the bond between children and their caregivers impacts their emotional and social growth. According to Bowlby, this attachment is a deep and enduring emotional bond that connects one person to another across time and space.

The theory proposes that children are born with a biological inclination to form attachments to enhance their chances of survival. Typically, the quality of the attachment formed is determined by how the caregiver meets the child's needs for security, comfort, and social connection.

When caregivers consistently respond and show sensitivity to a child's needs, a secure attachment is likely to develop. Securely attached children have the confidence to explore their surroundings, knowing they can count on their caregivers for safety and support.

If caregivers are emotionally unavailable or neglectful, children may develop insecure attachments. In adulthood, distinct types of insecure attachments, such as anxious, dismissive-avoidant and fearful-avoidant, can have unique characteristics and consequences for behaviour and relationships.

The "mother wound" and "father wound" explores the emotional and psychological scars we bear from our childhood attachments. These wounds aren't necessarily about gender; they're more about the roles our caregivers played.

A lack of nurturing, love and emotional connection often gives rise to the mother wound. It's like having an emptiness in your heart, desiring kind words, validation, cuddles and quality time that were never fully provided.

When your main source of support fails to make you feel truly seen and loved, as they should, it becomes a challenge. A mother wound can develop when a mother is emotionally unavailable, excessively critical or neglects to provide adequate care. This may result in self-worth issues, emotional management challenges and difficulties in forming healthy relationships.

Attachment theory indicates that the bond between mother and child starts to form at an incredibly young age.

Even in the womb, babies start to feel a sense of safety and security with their mothers. The absence or instability of that bond can also contribute to the mother wound.

In the same way, a father wound can emerge when a father is missing, uninterested or excessively judgmental. It could involve a lack of direction, security and feeling safe. The presence of an adult who instils confidence and guides us through life is invaluable.

The absence of a consistent paternal presence can leave you feeling disoriented and uncertain about setting boundaries or seeking support. It can produce a vacuum, a longing for a firm and supportive figure who could have offered stability and direction.

All genders can suffer from the father wound. Our self-worth, relationships and assertiveness are all influenced by it.

The difficulty lies in the fact that it's not necessarily about biological parents. It's about whoever was in your caregiver role. They may have had all the best intentions, but maybe they were overburdened or didn't understand how to provide precisely what you needed at that particular moment.

When we discuss the mother wound and father wound, we're essentially referring to emotional and psychological scars from childhood trauma, commonly caused by an unavailable or unattuned parent or caregiver. The profound impact of these attachment-related wounds can affect a person's ability to form secure relationships, their idea of self and their overall psychological well-being.

Bowlby's theory has had a profound influence on our understanding of the importance of early relationships. This has led to further research and therapeutic approaches for tackling attachment-related problems.

It's important to remember that, should these attachment challenges personally affect you, healing these wounds requires an iterative approach. It involves acknowledging the pain, reaching out for support, and gradually nurturing the wounded parts of yourself. You're not alone on this journey, and there are measures you can take to heal and find a healthier way forward.

It is also key for co-parents to consider the lengthy journey from infancy to adulthood. The events that transpire in between can greatly impact our ability to form close relationships as adults, as well as our early childhood experiences.

Finally, when looking at this from the perspective of how our own children experience our parenting of them, we can sometimes be tremendously disassociated or easily triggered and unable to provide the child what they need in the moment. This is completely valid and understandable. The attachment wounding is a result of a consistent lack of nurture or needs not being met over a prolonged period. Co-parents must remain kind and compassionate to themselves. We all sometimes get pushed to the edge.

The thing to remember in these scenarios is that the repair is key. Once the episode of stress is over, co-parents can sit down with the child, discuss what happened, and if needs be, apologise and ask for forgiveness. This approach can go a long way in helping children learn to manage conflict and repair.

You can gain insight into your own behaviours, as well as those of your children, by examining the attributes of different attachment types provided in Fig 3. It is important to note that these are general patterns and individual experiences can vary widely.

There are many online quizzes and resources that can guide you in discovering your primary attachment style. Support from therapists and counsellors can also help:

- **The Attachment Project's Free Attachment Style Test**: This test helps you determine if your attachment style is secure, anxious, avoidant, or disorganised: *quiz.attachmentproject.com*
- **Personal Development School's Attachment Style Quiz**: A quick quiz that provides a personalised report on your attachment style: *attachment.personaldevelopmentschool.com*
- **Best Personality Tests' Attachment Style Test**: This assessment covers secure, anxious, avoidant, and fearful attachment styles: *bestpersonalitytests.com/attachment-style-test*

These assessments can give you valuable insights into how you form emotional bonds and connections with others. As a note of reassurance, all attachments are workable to change and improve on to find the happy, healthy, and loving relationships we all deserve. It takes work and an honest look at ourselves, but with perseverance and courage, it all becomes worthwhile. The end results, from my own experiences, are nothing short of miraculous!

Attachment Style	Childhood Behaviours	Adult Behaviours
Secure	Comfortable with caregiver, upset when they leave but easily comforted upon return, confident to explore when caregiver is present	Comfortable with intimacy and independence, stable relationships, effective communication, trusts others
Anxious	Preoccupied. Very upset when caregiver leaves, not easily comforted upon return, seeks constant reassurance, clingy	Often worries about relationships, intensely seeks closeness, may be overly dependent, fears being alone
Dismissive-Avoidant	Indifference to caregiver's presence or absence, self-reliant, minimal emotional display	Values independence, avoids closeness, sees relationships as less important, has trust issues
Fearful-Avoidant	Mixed responses to caregiver's presence or absence, may show signs of confusion, duality of seeking and resisting closeness	Desires closeness but fears getting hurt, has trust issues, avoids intimacy while sometimes longing for it.

Fig 3: Some examples of different attachment styles, and possible corresponding behavioural outcomes

CHAPTER 17: THE LONG-TERM BENEFITS OF HARMONIOUS CO-PARENTING

The ultimate goal of co-parenting is to raise well-adjusted, happy children, despite the challenges of parenting from separate households. When parents build a harmonious co-parenting relationship, based on respect and cooperation, it can lead to significant long-term advantages for both parents and children. In this chapter, we investigate the long-lasting benefits and the positive ripple effects they can bring to the family's future.

The well-being of children greatly depends on stable and secure environments. Their emotional development relies on the consistency and predictability that a harmonious co-parenting relationship provides. Children who observe their parents cooperating amicably may experience reduced anxiety and stress associated with parental conflict. This fosters a sense of safety and belonging and supports the development of their own healthy emotional expression and conflict resolution skills. This stable environment allows children to develop a keen sense of trust and safety, which is crucial for their emotional well-being.

A supportive and cooperative co-parenting relationship fosters a positive self-image and confidence in children. When children see their parents working together and supporting each other, they feel valued and loved. This sense of worthiness boosts their self-esteem and encourages them to pursue their goals with confidence.

Children who grow up in a harmonious co-parenting environment are more likely to develop healthy emotional regulation skills. They learn how to manage their emotions effectively by observing their parents' positive interactions and conflict-resolution strategies. This ability to regulate emotions contributes to better mental health and resilience in the face of challenges. I'm sure we're all aware of the saying, "*Do as I do, not as I say*"—children learn through observation.

When co-parents maintain a cooperative relationship, they are teaching their children positive behaviour. Valuable life lessons can be taught to children through this. They can learn about the importance of respect and empathy in relationships, how to communicate and solve problems more effectively and how to better adapt to change and overcome adversity.

Co-parents can dedicate more attention to their own well-being and personal growth when conflict is absent, leading to decreased stress levels and improved mental health. With less conflict, more energy and attention can be directed toward parenting, and personal pursuits. This allows co-parents to enjoy a more fulfilling life after separation, with opportunities for new relationships and the exploration of brand-new or long-forgotten hobbies.

When co-parents have a harmonious relationship, it positively affects the broader family dynamic, including relationships with extended family and future partners. This provides children with a more extensive support system as a result. There would also be decreased tension at family gatherings and special occasions. The potential for strong and harmonious blended family dynamics also becomes a possibility.

The advantages of a cooperative co-parenting relationship can have a lasting impact on the children's adult relationships and their own parenting approach. It can give children a firmer grounding to establish their own healthy relationships. As well as this, if they have to endure similar circumstances, there is a higher chance of them co-parenting effectively having experienced it themselves. Our role as co-parents now can sustain positive family patterns to benefit future generations.

By placing cooperation and respect at the forefront, co-parents can build a legacy of stability, emotional health, and positive relationships for their children. Today's efforts to nurture a harmonious co-parenting atmosphere will resonate in the lives of their children, influencing their future and the family dynamics for years to come.

CHAPTER 18: REAL-LIFE SUCCESS STORIES OF CO-PARENTING

Sadly, I cannot authentically count myself in amongst this chapter—yet. I still have struggles in my own co-parenting dynamic and have authored this book as a call out to create the reality I believe my daughter needs from her co-parents. We are slowly integrating the child-centred approach, and the results have been significant. There are still some communication challenges however, and we still have a little way to go to complete harmony. Every day is an improvement though, and we are getting there. Forever united in unconditional love for our little girl, we are becoming better co-parents.

I have encountered some, though not many, co-parents who have found acceptance and relative peace in their dynamic, and I will share a couple of these here. It is worth noting that finding examples of success stories has been challenging, highlighting the epidemic that is happening in terms of difficult co-parenting stories. I have observed that those co-parenting relationships that are more harmonious are those where the couple has decided to split due to growing apart. There have been no betrayals or chaos. Perhaps this has a bearing on the type of relationship we end up having with our co-parent. However, the tools and techniques shared in this book are still applicable to all. Doing it for our kids, taking the plunge and being brave enough to face our true selves.

Hannah and Alan

Hannah and Alan have a four-year-old child and have been split up for two years. Their split was not amicable, and tensions were high as they broke agreements, shouted at each other in the street and forgot all about the love they had once shared. After a period of three weeks when Alan had no contact with either his soon-to-be ex-wife or child, a ceasefire was called. Hannah works as a child psychologist, supporting children through challenging times, and understood the importance of providing their daughter with security and emotional safety as her world split in two. Together she and Alan sat down and had a real think about what they thought would be best, not for them, but for her. They decided on an access schedule of 50/50 exactly and agreed on protocols and routines to be maintained between households. Initially, their relationship remained cool and distant, however, as their daughter developed and learnt to talk and express more, they began to see the joy on her face when they were together as a unit. Having this at the forefront of their minds, they began to have dinners together and go on family outings together and the change in their daughter was obvious. She became less reactive, more joyful, and more open to new experiences and people. Witnessing this solidified their resolve to co-parent more effectively. They agreed no new partners in their daughter's life and to keep her sense of stability a priority. Over time, they have become friends again, and now even go on holiday as a family. With strong boundaries around their own relationship, this has really worked for all of them, and their daughter continues to flourish.

Anna and Chris

Anna and Chris had two children, who were aged one and five, when Chris suddenly announced he wanted to leave Anna. Anna was completely blindsided and not prepared for this bombshell. She begged and drove herself crazy trying to win back his love, her self-esteem plummeting with each rejected attempt at reconciliation. After several rejections, and although still desperately wanting to work things out, she realised that Chris had emotionally left long before he told her. She decided to focus on herself by going to the gym, reading more, and taking care of her well-being. For the sake of stability, minimising disruption for their children became a new way for Anna and Chris to connect. Living close to the school their eldest attended, they decided not to split the children between two homes. Instead, they took turns moving in and out of the family home on alternate weeks. Chris bought a nearby flat, and Anna stayed with her mother when she had her week away from the children. Though strained, the friendship between the co-parents grew stronger, and the children adjusted well to this arrangement. This 'nesting' approach—keeping the children in the family home while the parents rotated—suited their dynamic well, allowing them to continue to function as a strong co-parenting unit.

In co-parenting, success is not always immediate, nor is it guaranteed. It takes time. Progress comes slowly. Setbacks are inevitable. But, as these stories show, when both parents commit to the child's well-being and maintain open communication, harmony can be achieved. These journeys remind us that it's possible to find a balance that works, even when the path to get there feels rocky and uncertain. The goal isn't perfection, but creating a space where the child can thrive—where love and security take priority. And for those of us still taking this journey with difficulties, there is hope that, with patience and effort, we too can find that balance.

PART III: THE ONWARD ADVENTURE

As we approach the last part of our co-parenting exploration, we understand that the journey continues beyond this guide. Co-parenting is a dynamic process that evolves alongside children's growth and changing family dynamics. In this concluding segment, we take a thoughtful glimpse into what lies ahead, encompassing aspirations, dreams, and an enduring pledge to prioritise the children's well-being in co-parenting. It serves as both a conclusion and a starting point. This statement acknowledges that while the formal guidance may come to an end, the co-parenting journey persists, filled with potential and promise. Co-parents are encouraged to look ahead with hope, dream confidently and keep building a future where their children can prosper. The adventure continues, offering co-parents the opportunity to build a legacy of love, stability, and growth for their family. As the author of *How Not To F*** Them Up*, Oliver James astutely remarks, "The real challenge of parenthood is you, not your child." For co-parents, the biggest challenge is us, not our children.

CHAPTER 19: LOOKING TO THE FUTURE—HOPES AND DREAMS

The future has a unique meaning for us as co-parents. It's not only a chronological sequence of upcoming events, but also a space to cultivate and nourish aspirations and goals for our children and ourselves. In this chapter, co-parents are encouraged to approach the future with optimism, set intentions and imagine the endless possibilities.

The primary focus for all parents is often the well-being and happiness of their children. Envisioning their future involves picturing their potential. Reflect on the desired future for your children. Discuss their interests and talents with them and explore ways to support their growth. Plan and discuss your children's educational and developmental goals, considering their ambitions and the necessary steps for success. These discussions can be with the children and the other co-parent or just the child themselves. Include them in conversations, listen to their own hopes and dreams and promote personal growth by providing a supportive environment for them to explore their identities, build resilience and cultivate independence.

As well as the children's bright futures, co-parents can also visualise what their own goals and aspirations with co-parenting are. When thinking ahead, it is important to establish co-parenting objectives. Make a constant effort to enhance communication and collaboration for the sake of your children. As your children mature, their requirements will evolve. Be ready to modify your co-parenting strategies accordingly. This is where the importance of self-awareness becomes increasingly more important. If a child says they do not want to go to the other parent or spend time with them, co-parents are encouraged to seek to understand the "*why*" rather than using coercion or force. Remember that the fight-flight-freeze response will be activated in the child who feels controlled. Sometimes children just need a break. It has no bearing on the love they have for their parent, and as adults, understanding this and acting accordingly with empathy, compassion, and a desire to understand can go a long way.

Plan for upcoming milestones, such as birthdays, graduations, or weddings, and determine how you'll celebrate them as co-parents. While the co-parenting experience is a joint effort, individual aspirations are equally valued. Encourage each other to follow personal interests and goals, understanding that individual happiness is vital for the family's overall well-being. Promote each other's career growth, recognising that success in this realm can bring stability and opportunities for the family. Stay open to the potential of new relationships and navigating blended family dynamics, approaching these changes with sensitivity and thoughtfulness for all parties. Visualising hopes and dreams when deep in co-parenting conflict, or not, can sometimes seem a bit of an overwhelming task. Some ideas for how to make it practical and enjoyable are:

- **Vision boards:** A vision board is a collage of images, words and items that represent aspirations and desires. Physical vision boards can be created using magazines, photos and art supplies, or digital tools like Pinterest, Canva or Instagram are some ways to create a digital vision board.
- **Mood boards:** Like vision boards, mood boards are collections of textures, colours and images that convey a particular feeling or aspiration.
- **Mental rehearsal:** Close your eyes and vividly imagine yourself achieving your goals. Picture every detail, including the sights, sounds and emotions associated with your success.
- **Affirmations:** Pair your visualisations with positive affirmations. Repeating statements like "I am at peace" or "I am conflict-free" can reinforce your mental images and boost your confidence.
- **Daily practice:** Set aside a few minutes each day to practice visualisation. Consistency is key to making this technique effective.
- **Writing on index cards**: Write your goals and dreams on index cards or notecards and review them regularly. This can help reinforce your intentions and keep you focused.
- **Living in the moment:** Act as if your dreams have already come true. This mindset can help you align your actions with your goals and attract the opportunities you need.

Co-parenting, just like life, is always changing. Co-parents are encouraged to embrace the evolution and the reality that the co-parenting dynamic will transform, and they must be ready to adapt accordingly.

Plan for significant changes, whether it's a child going off to university or a parent moving to a new location. Stay united as co-parents, always prioritising the children's needs regardless of what the future brings and how their needs may impact your own sense of worth or safety. Co-parents can shape a future that satisfies both their children's needs and their own aspirations through goal setting, personal growth, and readiness for change. Co-parenting is a never-ending adventure that unfolds with each new chapter in life.

This was never in our grand plan as we set out on the parenting journey and, for me, it has taken a while to adapt. None of us have the rulebook, everybody is different, and we were once deeply in love with our co-parent (in most instances). Remembering this can help navigate some of these troubled waters. Life has a way of working itself out, and these challenges provide powerful learning opportunities—not only to bring us closer to our children and their other parent but also to connect us more deeply with the essence of our true selves.

CHAPTER 20: CONCLUDING THOUGHTS AND REFLECTIONS

As we wrap up this guide, this final chapter provides a space for us to contemplate and appreciate the co-parenting journey. This is a moment for introspection, acknowledging the achievements, the knowledge and wisdom acquired, and the resilience fostered throughout the long and winding path. Dedicated to the love and perseverance of all co-parents, this conclusion highlights the profound impact we have on our children's lives.

The path of co-parenting is paved with both successes and obstacles. As co-parents, we can gain insights by reflecting on our journey and recognising the growth that comes from co-parenting, both on a personal and relational level. Each experience is an opportunity to gain wisdom. Each challenge overcome is a lesson for future interactions and decisions.

Often, we forget, or don't take the time to really understand, that the effort exerted in co-parenting is priceless for the children's well-being, even if it goes unacknowledged. The co-parenting journey, despite its complexity, is invaluable. Although perhaps not the desired route, focusing on the positives can greatly enhance the overall reality. Children can benefit greatly from co-parenting, as it gives them love, guidance and stability from both parents, shaping their foundation in life. The journey for the co-parents promotes self-discovery, communication skills, and a better grasp of compromise and collaboration. Finally, the overall co-parenting relationship has a profound impact on the entire family, including relationships with extended family and future partners.

As co-parents advance in their growth, they are reminded that the contribution of a co-parent is crucial in shaping a child's life and future. Support is within reach—there is a community of assistance, encompassing both personal connections and experts, on standby to provide aid when needed. Regardless of familial situations, co-parents are reminded that there are communities on hand to offer a listening ear, offer practical support and help you see that you are not alone. As marriages crumble at an ever-increasing rate, co-parenting is becoming more common—there is always someone who can hold your hand as and when you need it.

We are all urged to remember: *there is no definitive endpoint to the ongoing journey of co-parenting.* So, we may as well attempt to make the best of it, whether that is through the relationship with the co-parent, or with yourself.

Co-parents design the future, transforming it into a landscape of possibilities. We must all endeavour to embrace the unknown and stay open to possibilities by adapting with an open heart, always basing decisions on the children's best interests. This is not easy! Make sure to honour achievements and value moments of connection and happiness.

In summary, this is an acknowledgement of the significance of the co-parenting path. It honours the bravery needed to navigate this journey and acknowledges the love that guides every choice, discussion, and concession. Co-parents can find reassurance in knowing that their commitment to co-parenting is an invaluable gift to their children's future. As the journey unfolds, so does the chance to shape a legacy filled with love and understanding for generations to follow.

This book has been a labour of love—a testament to the journey that so many of us now face. I genuinely believe that if more people knew and understood the realities of co-parenting then perhaps divorce rates would be lower, more relationships would be worked on, and people would think more consciously before starting a parenting journey. I wanted to put my perspective down on paper as a legacy for my daughter, and to provide a guide to those who may be struggling to make sense of it all. I genuinely am the best version of myself I have ever been. My co-parenting experience has pushed me to depths of myself I never knew existed, and I am grateful. I am a better parent as a result, and I am proud to share my experiences with the world. Thank you for reading my book. I hope it has helped you to feel more positive about where you find yourselves and how to continue to move forward with grace, compassion and understanding for yourselves, as well as those involved in your co-parenting dynamic.

With love, thanks, and praise to all who have supported me, including my co-parent, without whom, this book would not have manifested into reality. Ever grateful.

REFERENCES

- Bowlby, J. (1969). *Attachment: Attachment and Loss.* London: Pelican Books.
- Department for Work & Pensions. (2024). *Separated families statistics: April 2014 to March 2023.* [Online]. GOV.UK. Last Updated: 21 March 2024. Available at: https://www.gov.uk/government/statistics/separated-families-statistics-april-2014-to-march-2023/separated-families-statistics-april-2014-to-march-2023 [Accessed 4 September 2024].
- Greene, R. (2018) 'Chapter 2', in The Laws of Human Nature. Profile Books, pp. 29–34.
- James, O. (2011). *How Not to F*** Them Up.* London: Vermillion.
- Jung, C. (1973). *Letters.* 2nd ed. New Jersey: Princeton University Press. p.33.
- Kozlowska, K. MBBS, FRANZCP, PhD; Walker, P. BSc Psych, MPsychol *et al.* (2015). Fear and the Defense Cascade: Clinical Implications and Management. *Harvard Review of Psychiatry.* 23(4), pp.263-287. [Online]. Available at: https://journals.lww.com/hrpjournal/Fulltext/2015/07000/Fear_and_the_Defense_Cascade__Clinical.3.aspx [Accessed 4 September 2024].

- Kruk, E. PhD. (2012). *Co-Parenting and High Conflict: Separating Former Marital Disputes from Ongoing Parenting Responsibilities.* [Online]. Psychology Today. Last Updated: 15 May 2012. Available at: www.psychologytoday.com/intl/blog/co-parenting-after-divorce/201205/co-parenting-and-high-conflict [Accessed 4 September 2024].
- Maté, G. (2019). *When the Body Says No: The Cost of Hidden Stress.* London: Vermillion.
- Micheletti, M. and Cottrell, A. (2019). *The Inner Work: An Invitation to True Freedom and Lasting Happiness.* United States: Independently Published.
- Robert Greene, *The Laws of Human Nature*, Chapter 2 P29 - 34
- Sarno, J. E. (2010). *Healing Back Pain: The Mind-Body Connection.* London: Wellness Central.
- Spencer, L. (2024). *Narcissistic personality disorder (NPD) – signs, causes, and impact.* [Online]. Rest Less. Last Updated: 3 June 2024. Available at: https://restless.co.uk/health/healthy-mind/narcissistic-personality-disorder-npd-signs-causes-and-impact/ [Accessed 4 September 2024].
- Stixrud, W. PhD and Johnson, N. (2018). *The Self-Driven Child: The Science and Sense of Giving Your Kids More Control Over Their Lives.* New York: Viking.
- United Nations, Department of Economic and Social Affairs, Population Division (2024). *World Population Prospects 2024.* Available at: https://data.unicef.org/how-

many/how-many-children-under-18-are-there-in-the-uk/ [Accessed: 4 September 2024].

- Villafuerte, V. (2023). *Study reveals types of positive childhood experiences (PCEs) linked to improved mental and physical health outcomes in adulthood.* [Online]. UCLA Health. Last Updated: 8 December 2023. Available at: https://www.uclahealth.org/news/release/study-reveals-types-positive-childhood-experiences-pces [Accessed 4 September 2024].
- White, W. MC CMHC, NCC, LPC. (2020). *Narcissistic Personality Disorder: DSM-5 Criteria And Treatment Options.* [Online]. Mind Diagnostics. Last Updated: 5 November 2020. Available at: https://www.mind-diagnostics.org/blog/narcissistic-personality/narcissistic-personality-disorder-dsm-5-criteria-and-treatment-options [Accessed 4 September 2024].
- *Fight, flight, or freeze response: Signs, causes, and recovery* https://www.medicalnewstoday.com/articles/fight-flight-or-freeze-response [Accessed 5 September 2024]